Cardinal
Feathers
gifts from my son's life....
and death by suicide

by
Diane Simon

Bloomington, IN Milton Keynes, UK

authorHOUSE

AuthorHouse™
1663 Liberty Drive, Suite 200
Bloomington, IN 47403
www.authorhouse.com
Phone: 1-800-839-8640

AuthorHouse™ UK Ltd.
500 Avebury Boulevard
Central Milton Keynes, MK9 2BE
www.authorhouse.co.uk
Phone: 08001974150

This book is a work of non-fiction. Unless otherwise noted, the author and the publisher make no explicit guarantees as to the accuracy of the information contained in this book and in some cases, names of people and places have been altered to protect their privacy.

First published by AuthorHouse 5/9/2006

ISBN: 1-4259-2128-0 (e)
ISBN: 1-4259-2127-2 (sc)

Printed in the United States of America
Bloomington, Indiana

This book is printed on acid-free paper.

Dedication

I dedicate this book to you, dear, dear Cale, for you live in every beat of my heart; in every thought that passes through my mind; in every word that I speak and every breath that I take.

I feel you with me always and thank God for opening my mind to the knowledge and belief that we do not need to exist in the same life vibration to be connected.

Be at peace my beloved son, and know that I love you more than words can ever say. I will hold you in my heart, until the day I can once again hold you in my arms.

I dedicate this also to you, Adam, my incredible, wonderful son. You are my world, and I love you more than you will ever know, ferociously and eternally. I am so proud of the young man that you have become. Forever, you will own my heart in a way no one else can.

And to you, Brad, my amazing husband. I have watched as you have grown to become an incredible, wonderful father and husband, and I am in awe of how very hard you worked to bring about positive change in your life. You have walked with me on life's paths for more than 25 years, and dodged potholes and falling rock, mudslides and washouts, hurricanes and tornadoes. You truly are my soul mate and I am eternally gratefully that you are a part of my life. I love you.

Ange – I would not, could not love you more if you truly were my daughter.

Joanne – words cannot express my love and gratitude....

**Some names have been changed for reasons of personal privacy. These names are marked with a double asterisk.

Introduction

Simon, Cale Joseph, 16 years...at his home in Cottam.

How peaceful these words sounded; how innocuous and harmless.

Yet how these words have haunted me since they appeared in my son's obituary. How many times I have wanted to go back and change them, re-write them, 'truth' them.

Cale didn't die peacefully or innocuously. He didn't die suddenly. His death was agonizingly long and the road tortured by high mountains and deep pits; the brightest of lights and the blackest darkness – peaks and valleys all forged of mental illness.

He found peace only after death. He chose to end what had become for him an unbearable, unlivable, unlovable life.

In the months following his death, I had only one regret. I had not chosen to tell the truth in his obituary. Telling the truth would have helped to take away the stigma of suicide and mental illness that so many people continue to face today. Telling the truth would have shown my acceptance of my son's decision – and I did accept it, totally, with an understanding that only I, as his mother, could have.

I can't go back, but I can commit to telling the truth from this point on. I can commit, as I did to Cale a few months prior to his death

– to continuing to tell the truth and to fight for change, tolerance and acceptance, and access to proper and appropriate diagnosis and treatment for children with mental health challenges. I can commit to continuing to fight for change for children and adults – for children with mental illness grow up to become adults with mental illness. It is only in the telling the truth that we, as a society, and I, as a mother will find a way to change the overwhelming tide of people, young and old, who are completing suicide as a way of ending the pain and suffering of life. It is only in telling the truth that I, as Cale's mother, can keep my promise to him.

And it is only in telling Cale's story, and mine, that I can reach out to others in the hope of making a difference.

To the other families – mothers, fathers, sisters, brothers, sons, daughters, grandparents, cousins, aunts, uncles – who have lost a loved one to suicide, my greatest wish is that through this book you realize you are not alone, you are not crazy, you are not at fault. There is help available to you, if you choose to reach out. You will survive. Know also, that if you are open, there will be gifts. It is hard to choose to be open; to choose to believe that something good might come from your loved one's death. But it can be, and the gifts are often amazing and life saving.

Should this book end up in the hands of teenagers and youth who struggle for acceptance, for love, for guidance, for peace – reach out for help. Find someone to talk to, anyone. If you can't get help with the first person you turn to, try someone else – a teacher, a friend's parents, a librarian, a coffee shop waitress, a counselor at a local agency, a police officer, a friend. Just reach out and live. Suicide is not the answer. It is not the answer for you, and it truly is not the answer for those you leave behind, who are faced with a lifetime of missing you, questioning why and wondering 'what if.' If you read this book you will know that suicide destroys lives – more than just the life of the person who completes the act. Suicide is like a tsunami – it hits without warning, with incredible, unforeseeable force destroying everything in its path on impact, and for years, sometimes generations to come. Survivors of suicide live forever with the consequences of that decision.

If you are a teenager or young adult, and you know someone who is struggling with suicidal thoughts, suicidal ideation, or has attempted suicide, tell someone! This is an incredibly hard secret to bear when your friend is alive; it will become even harder if your friend completes suicide. Telling someone is the kindest, most loving gesture you can make, even though it may feel like betrayal at the time. Don't assume that the person is just looking for attention – many lives have been lost because of this assumption. So tell someone; your mom, dad, sister, brother, a friend, clergy, social worker, teacher – anyone you can think of who might be able to help.

To those who work in the field of children's mental health, please, listen to your hearts. A child's mental health problems are not always just behavioural! Listen to the parents as well, for they know their children best. Be open to the possibilities.

If you are reading this book and you have attempted suicide in the past, read carefully and try to truly understand what happens to those who are left behind. And reach out for help. It is available. It may not always be easy to find and 'doing the work' to get well may be the hardest thing you will ever do, but it is worth it. Just reach out for help.

You may have picked this book up for any other reason – the title caught your attention, the cover caught your eye or the book fell off the shelf in front of you and you therefore believe you were meant to read it. My greatest prayer for you is that after completing the book you will have a greater understanding and awareness of suicide, children's and adult mental illness, societal stigma and the need for tolerance, understanding, compassion and assistance for both those who complete suicide and those who are left behind. Know that life is short and precious and much of it is out of our control. If this book causes you to look at your own relationships, and allows you to see them differently, to see where changes can be made and connections can be strengthened, then follow your heart. You know what to do.

Chapter One

The day my son died, invisible hands descended from the skies, grabbing the corners of my world and turning it upside down. My life was shaken violently, torn from its very foundation. Pieces of my life broke loose with an unstoppable force, filling the sky like snow in a snow globe. When my world finally settled back on its foundation, everything had shifted. All the pieces existed, but nothing remained where it had been.

In the months, weeks, days....sometimes mere moments that followed, I began shoveling the debris, one heavy heap at a time, looking for the former paths of my life. It took quite some time for me to realize those paths were gone, destroyed like pathways in an avalanche. But the shovel remained in my hands. Somewhere, deep inside my very soul, I knew that I could choose to build new paths, new roadways, if I desired.

And so I began to dig.

Chapter Two

Cale was 16 years old when he chose to end his life. It had been a difficult life, filled with mental illness and an ongoing brutal effort to access help and treatment. It had been a life of struggle – struggle to fit in, to be accepted, to be understood, to understand.

But shortly before he died, Cale had turned a corner...or so we thought. A new medication seemed to be working. I was seeing more of the sweetness and compassion, the humour and intelligence that resided in Cale, and less of the sadness, volatility and rage. Late winter headed for spring, which was just around the corner. At the same time Cale, I thought, was heading for a spring of his own.

April 7, 2003 was one of those winter days that even winter lovers hate. It had been preceded by some lovely pre-spring days that made people anxious for what was to come – sunshine, warm weather and rebirth.

Mother Nature, or perhaps Old Man Winter, had different plans for winter's final hoorah, however. That April Monday brought with it snow, sleet, rain, freezing rain, wind...a little of everything. My oldest son, Adam, was in Belle River at the home of his girlfriend, Ange, and her parents. Although I can't remember, I assume my husband Brad, was probably up and working in the garage when I left for work. He worked afternoons as a truck mechanic at TST Overland at the time. Likewise, I assume I drove Cale to school – Leamington District Secondary School – that morning, although I can't really remember. That was the normal routine. I would drive him to school, stopping for a 'Timmy's' - a coffee for him and a tea for me at Tim Horton's on the way. Although he was supposed to take the bus, he hated it. To be truthful, I didn't push the issue much as I enjoyed the time with him in the morning before I headed to my job in Windsor.

When I dropped him off at school, the routine was always the same. Cale would head to the southeast corner of the property where a big cement block was located. There he would meet a couple friends – Kelly Hutchins, Mike Hicks and a few others – and sitting on the cement block, share a cigarette or two before heading in.

I imagine this is what happened April 7 but as much as I try, I can't quite remember. I do know I headed in to work at Windsor Essex Family Network. I had just recently returned to work after having had lower back surgery in January. After arriving I was quickly caught up in the details of running a workshop we were hosting that day.

I had left my cell phone in my car and I wasn't able to check messages during the day. By the time I left the workshop around 5 p.m. to head for home, Cale had left several messages. I listened to them anxiously, knowing that although Cale had been fine that morning, things could change quickly with his moods, anxieties and worries. If anything, however, Cale sounded happy and excited on the messages, urging me to call him as soon as I got the messages, which I did. He had updated his resume and was preparing a list of all the golf clubs in Windsor and Essex County, in order to apply for a summer job. He wanted my help in preparing the cover letter. I was proud of him and called to tell him so, and to let him know I was on my way home. I reminded him I would be a few minutes longer because of the icy roads.

For me, Cale's interest in finding a job was the latest sign that things might be turning around for him. About six weeks earlier he had started taking Lithium for Bipolar Disorder. While he had been treated for many years for the condition, Brad and I had seen more positive results from this medication than any of the others. These positive changes came on the heels of a very difficult year for Cale, and the rest of our family. So I headed home that day, happy for Cale and grateful for these positive changes. What I didn't know, had no way of knowing, was he was in a manic phase of his illness – a 'high' that made it absolutely necessary, in his mind, for him to get all 30 or so of these resumes out that day; a 'high' that would make the crash that was to follow even more severe.

When I arrived home I helped Cale prepare the letter and envelopes for the resumes. We faxed those we had fax numbers for, and prepared the rest for mailing. Cale then headed downstairs to put up a shelf in his room. Struggling with a nasty headache that had plagued me all day, I sat down to relax. A short time later I heard a loud bang, followed by swearing, coming from Cale's room. Going downstairs, I found Cale struggling to put up the shelf in the corner of his room. His high frustration level was obvious to me – I was well aware of the signs. After watching him continue to struggle and swear for a few moments, I suggested it might be good for him to take a break and go out for a breath of fresh air.

The words were no sooner out of my mouth when Cale turned towards me and wheeled the hammer across the room. It soared passed my head, close enough that I felt the rush of air before it struck the wall about two feet away from me, leaving a large hole. Cale had always promised that he would never hurt me, know matter how angry or out of control he became. So as the hammer struck the wall, I felt no fear. It was beyond my comprehension to believe that Cale would purposely try to hurt me. I made a mental decision to talk to Cale about the incident later, when he had calmed down. In the time since Cale's death I have come to realize this was one of the few moments when I might have made a difference. I chose instead to ask him again to take a break.

I will never forget the look in Cale's eyes, or the words he spoke – the last words he would ever say to me. I could see in his eyes that he was horrified by what he had just done. The emotions flashed across his face. I wanted to tell him it was okay; that I knew he had not intended to hurt me. But I also knew he had to hear that intent or not, he could have hurt me. I said nothing.

Cale's eyes went flat as he put down the shelf and other things he was holding. He reached out, grabbed his cigarettes off the top of the dresser and looked at me, his shoulders sagging.

"You're right, it's time for me to go," he said to me, the pain in his voice as obvious as the hole in the wall next to me.

Cale walked passed me, out the door of his room and out the back door, lighting a cigarette. I watched him go, wearing only a t-shirt, and figured he would have a cigarette, get some fresh air and come back in. Still battling my headache, I decided to lay down for 15 minutes while he was outside, and talk to him later. Our German Shepherd, Chelsea, curled up on the bed beside me.

About a half hour later I opened my eyes to a quiet house. Knowing that Chelsea would have barked if Cale come back into the house; and knowing that Cale had wore only a t-shirt when he left, I jumped up from the bed fighting the panic that immediately rose in my throat.

Having just had back surgery two months earlier, I made my way as quickly as possible down the stairs, calling Cale's name. He was not in his room or the main part of the house, as I suspected considering Chelsea's silence. Sticking my head out the door I peered through the sleet, snow and freezing rain. There was no sign of Cale, and no response to my calls.

Panic rising in my throat, I called Brad at work. Although worried, Brad reminded me that Cale often went for walks to calm down and think. Wearing only a t-shirt, he couldn't be too far. I promised to call him as soon as Cale returned home.

I also took some small comfort in knowing Cale may have grabbed an extra sweatshirt or coat from the van, where they seemed to gather.

The minutes that followed are at times fuzzy and dim, and at other times as clear and precise as cut crystal. I headed outside with a flashlight to walk around our large back yard, certain I would see Cale huddled out of the wind with a cigarette, or sitting in my husband's shop or the back garage. With each location I checked there was no sign of Cale. My anxiety and fear grew, and panic threatened to take over.

I called Brad to let him know I was going for a drive around the block – an entire concession and the sideroads that bordered it – in case Cale had decided to walk. I could hear the tension and worry in Brad's voice as he told me to take my cell phone, and call him.

I headed out slowly driving west from my house, down our road, up a sideroad, down the next concession and another sideroad. I wondered if he could be laying in a ditch, having been hit by a vehicle, but I had no way of knowing. And there was no sign of him.

Then, as I approached our house from the east, I noticed the light shining in our bathroom.

And I knew. I knew that if Cale was in the bathroom, then he had purposely snuck in quietly enough not to arouse the dog – a pretty significant feat. And I knew that there could only be one reason he would do this.

These thoughts flashed through my mind in a split second, and just as quickly I banished them, telling myself to stop. I think I called Brad from the van as I approached the house, but I'm not sure. I think I told him the light was on in the bathroom. I think. I'm not sure.

What I do know is I parked the van and raced into the house, throwing open the door to the bathroom without even knocking. The image of my son hanging from the top of the shower stall, an electrical cord tied around his neck, struck me like a freight train, snatching the air from my lungs. His eyes were closed, his lips were blue and his limbs were limp. Somewhere in the back of my mind I knew that I was too late, but I remember a surge of denial, a surge of belief that I could save him, wash over me like a tidal wave. I had to; I was his mother! I raced for the telephone to call 9-1-1 and raced back to the bathroom, frantically dialing while holding the phone between my shoulder and ear as I tried to lift Cale up to lessen the tension so I could undo the cord. Unable to lift his 180 pound frame high enough to ease the tension, I dropped the phone. I could hear the 9-1-1 dispatcher talking to me in the background as I used both arms to lift him up and reach up to the cord. Pain scorched through my lower back at the surgery site, and I ignored it, wanting only to save my son. Unable to loosen the cord enough to undo it, I grabbed scissors out of the drawer and again lifted Cale up – this time in an effort to keep his body from striking the floor when I cut the cord. I didn't want him hurt anymore than he already was. Again the pain raced through my back, this time bringing hot tears to my eyes, and again I ignored it, cutting the cord and lowering Cale to the floor, where I struggled to untie the knot holding the remaining piece of cord around his neck. Trying hard to fight the panic and emotion; knowing I was the only one home, I tried desperately to remember my former CPR training - wishing I had kept my certification up to date - while I listened to the 9-1-1 operator.

For what seemed liked hours, but was only mere minutes, I performed CPR and mouth to mouth resuscitation on my son. The emergency operator talked to me constantly, coaching me and telling me how well I was doing. The phone kept slipping from its cradle on my shoulder as I struggled to do compressions. Chelsea whimpered beside me, sensing that something was not right, and trying to get to Cale's face to lick him.

Each time I blew into Cale's lungs the breath bubbled back out with an unnatural whoosh sound, quickly, as if it had hit a brick wall. I fought the urge to put my hand over his mouth…to hold the breath in his lungs. I pleaded with him, begged him to breath. At one point I stopped compressions and placed my hand on his chest, praying to feel his heart beat beneath my hand. At another point I stopped to try to rub away the marks on his neck where the cord had been embedded, before returning to the compressions.

When the police and ambulance personnel arrived, everything began to happen quickly, yet slowly…in a sort of surreal fog. Police officers arrived first and I was ushered from the bathroom to make room for the emergency workers. Officer **Bill Chalmers took charge of Chelsea, who was agitated and anxious, not understanding what was happening to her family. It was obvious Officer Chalmers liked and was comfortable with dogs. He calmed and walked her around the house - even taking the time to discover where we kept her treats - until a friend arrived later and took over. I took comfort in knowing that my beautiful dog, who is anxious, high strung and suffers from separation anxiety as a result of puppy hood abuse, was in good hands.

I sat on the stairwell beside the bathroom as paramedics worked on Cale. Officer **Sharon Cook had tried to bring me upstairs, but I didn't want to be that far away from Cale, and she didn't push. Instead she stayed with me, on the stairwell, as activity swirled around us like a tornado.

I called my sister Joanne, my best friend, and despite having just undergone open heart surgery two months earlier, she assured me she would be right there. I called my brother Norm, who also said he would come right over.

In the ensuing moments more police officers arrived. I lost count of how many officers and emergency workers filled my house. Everywhere I looked there were uniforms. Red lights from the police cars and ambulances flashed through my house, over and over, for what seemed like hours. I felt the flashes pulse through my head and my body like electricity, and wondered if I was dreaming. Everything was so unreal.

As I waited for 'official word' of what I already knew, I talked to the police officers about my husband. I couldn't call him. I knew he was worried and waiting for a phone call, but I couldn't face the thought of having to tell him what had happened. Parenting Cale had been a huge challenge, and Brad had found the struggle more difficult and complex than I. In the last few years, however, Brad had been working hard to understand Cale's illness, and was concentrating on building a new, positive relationship with Cale. It seemed so unfair now, to tell him it was over. I was terrified that if I called him to tell him that his son might now be dead, was dead, he would race home on the icy roads. I was terrified of losing him too, on the 45 minute drive home.

I don't know if I asked, or if it was just offered, but within moments Officer Tim James was telling me not to worry...he would go get Brad and drive him home. Kindness radiated from his eyes, and relief flooded through me, knowing that Brad would be safe with this man.

It wasn't long before paramedics emerged from my bathroom, without my son. Someone told me he was gone. Someone said 'I'm sorry." I didn't care. I just wanted to see him.

Someone, Officer Cook I believed, warned me that Cale would have a tube in his throat. I heard the voice explaining that although it was believed that he was dead when paramedics arrived, they had to continue trying to save him, because I had already started the process by carrying out CPR and mouth to mouth resuscitation. Once in, the tubes and IV lines had to stay until the coroner arrived.

I didn't care. I just wanted to be left alone with my son.

When I entered the bathroom Cale was laying flat on the floor on his back, surrounded by IV tubing, wrappings, syringe caps and other debris from the previous hours. I crossed the room, knelt on the floor beside him and laid my cheek against his forehead. And cried. Hot tears ran across my cheeks and onto Cale's face, traveling across the cool skin to fall on my hand, which held the side of his face. With my other hand I tried again to rub out the indentations in his neck, willing the angry blue and red marks to disappear.

His skin was cool, cooler than it had been when I found him. He was still, so very, very still. Unimaginably still for Cale, who was always moving, even when he wasn't moving…whose head or legs or hands were always moving.

And he was peaceful, something I had not seen in a very, very long time.

It was this thought that filled my head when my sister arrived and dropped to the ground with me. I remember asking her if I was a bad mother because I was grateful that Cale was at peace. Joanne knew as well as anyone what Cale's struggles had been. She said no, tears streaming down her face.

I don't know how long I sat in the bathroom with Cale, but when Brad arrived I felt what little control I had left shatter into a million pieces, scattering in all directions. He dropped to the floor beside me and I grabbed on to him like a lifeline, sobbing uncontrollably. In the midst of my own grief I felt his shoulders heaving beneath the heavy winter jacket he wore as sobs tore through his body. It was the only time I could remember my husband crying in more than 20 years. I don't know how long we sat holding each other, sitting beside the lifeless body of our son.

At some point we were ushered out of the room and paramedics prepared to take Cale's body away. Joanne called Ange's parents to let Adam know what had happened. Ange's father Dennis told Joanne he would drive them home.

Norm and my sister-in-law Kathy arrived shortly after Brad. I would find out later that the cruiser with Officer James and Brad in it raced passed them on the way, and Norm and Kathy knew immediately where it was heading. I called my sister-in-law Brenda, Brad's twin sister, with the news. I remember apologizing for having to tell her over the phone, and asking her to walk next door to tell Brad's parents. They arrived within minutes.

Somehow my mother was also notified, I'm not sure by whom. Joanne's boyfriend Glenn went to pick her up and she arrived with her brother D'Arcy. A representative from Victims Services arrived. In fact, she was one of the first people to arrive. She spend the evening making herself available – quietly and unobtrusively - to anyone who might need to talk, and left me with information I would later read, and use in my healing process.

As the evening progressed, reality and surrealism mixed. For much of the evening I felt like I was dreaming – floating in some weird twilight and viewing the scene from someone else's eyes. Then I would snap back to reality in a moment. One such moment occurred when I turned to see Adam and Ange, having just arrived, rushing across the dining room to reach Brad and I. Clutching each other close the four of us sobbed as if we were the only ones in the room. For Ange, who had been a part of Adam's, and our lives, for two years, it was just as hard. Cale had been like a brother to her. In fact, Ange was often the only one who could calm him down when he became upset, with himself in particular.

Standing there, locked in a frantic embrace with my oldest son, a very different and significant reality set in. I simply could not deny the reality that my youngest son was gone while my oldest son sobbed in my arms.

I had not seen Adam cry for many, many years. I knew how very much it took to make him cry.

Cale was taken away and Brad and I were taken upstairs to talk to Inspector **Gary Harper, who was on duty that evening. I found out later that during this time Joanne and Kathy cleaned up the bathroom, not wanting Brad and I to have to do this. Later Joanne and Adam were down in Cale's bedroom while another police officer investigated. Seeing the music posters on the wall, the officer made a remark about Cale's death and the music he listened. The tone of the remark insinuated Brad and I, as parents, should have known this would happen when we allowed him to listen to the music he chose.

Angry, Joanne tried to explain that Cale's music was just that – music. It wasn't who he was. She would later tell me how she tried to explain who Cale really was; how kind and compassionate he could be, how when he entered a room he filled it, how his smile could light your heart in an instant, how he wasn't a sum of the music he liked to listen to. She would later tell me how it seemed like her words were falling on deaf ears; that this officer had his mind made up, even though he had never met Cale. Joanne spent the rest of the night running interference to make sure Brad and I weren't alone with this officer. She didn't want him repeating his words to us.

Adam was angry too, and would later tell me how hard it was to hold his temper. Adam knew better than anyone that Cale wasn't a saint…that life with Cale was difficult and volatile and passionate. But he knew the other side of Cale as well, and he knew Cale's death wasn't because of the music we 'let' him listen to.

At some point during the evening a friend, Linda, and her boyfriend Roger arrived at our house. I don't know how they found out about Cale, or who called them. It may have been me, but I don't remember calling. In the two years since his death I have learned there is much I do not remember. Cale and Linda were very close and Cale often visited Linda's home. Roger and Cale had recently entered a pact in which Cale agreed to remove all his piercings – of which there were many - and Roger was going to get a tattoo with him. Cale had been scheduled to get the tattoo the following Saturday.

Once Cale's body was taken away and the police left, an eerie quiet descended upon the house. The flashing red of the lights was gone and people slowly started to leave, their reluctance to leave Brad and I alone evident. I began to allow myself to think that maybe I imagined everything, but the red eyes and drawn faces of those around me was a stark reminder that I had not.

Adam and Ange headed back to Ange's house in Belle River. I would soon realize that this would be the official 'moving out' point for Adam. Up to this time he and Ange had spent some time at our home and some at hers, depending on what shifts each of them was scheduled to work. After Cale's death, however, they pretty well stayed in Belle River. While I could understand, it was heartbreaking for me. I learned, without time for preparation, what 'empty nest syndrome' truly meant. Before it had only been a term I read about or heard used; now it was my life, and it felt like I had lost both my sons.

Brad and I went to bed that night – or rather early Tuesday morning - holding each other tight and trying to understand what had happened. The house was eerily quiet after the noise and confusion of the past hours. Chelsea stuck close to us, knowing that something had changed, but not knowing what.

Sleep eluded us, but by morning we had made a few important decisions – Cale's funeral would be a celebration of his life and we would stick together...making decisions together. We had been through enough in our lives and our marriage to know that trauma can easily destroy marriages. We were determined that Cale's death would bring us closer together rather than farther apart.

I left home early the next morning to visit the high school. I didn't want any of Cale's friends to hear about his death on the radio or through rumour or gossip. I spoke to vice principal **Bob Tells, well aware that only days earlier I had talked with Mr. Tells about how good Cale seemed to be doing. This day, I left the school with the contents of Cale's locker in my arms, hoping eventually to find some answers hidden there.

I then visited Ida Forbes, who had babysat my boys for many years while I worked. Ida was like a mother to my sons. I didn't want her hearing on the radio either.

My next stop was at the home of my friend Claire Bondy, a youth minister. Cale had attended grade school with her daughter Crissandra. Although Cale had struggled with religion and his personal beliefs for many years, he respected Claire and her husband Tim, who had always welcomed him with open arms and accepted him into their home. There were only two 'church' representatives Brad and I had considered for Cale's funeral service. Cale had really liked and respected Father John Duarte, another very good friend of mine. Father John however, was out of the country at the time. Brad and I had decided during the night to ask Claire to 'officiate' at Cale's funeral. I never considered what we would do if Claire had said no. She didn't.

The next few days were filled with calling friends and family and planning for Cale's funeral. As we faced decisions and issues no parent should have to face, we were grateful for the guidance of our brother-in-law John, who is married to Brad's oldest sister Judy, and who happens to be, by profession, a funeral director. John did not work at the funeral home we had chosen for Cale, but was able to step in to assist us with many of responsibilities and decisions Brad and I were facing. Years of experience, coupled with the closeness of family and his own private grief over losing his nephew, provided him with a unique knowledge of what we were dealing with, and how very overwhelmed Brad and I were. Working with our funeral director, Kevin Reid at Reid Funeral Home in Leamington, John provided a wall of support as Brad and I were faced with one decision after another in preparing for the funeral of our son. One of the most important, for me, was the preparation of Cale's body. I was struggling with the image of Monday night stuck in my mind and John knew how very badly I needed to see Cale again, to replace that image. John prepared Cale's body, then brought Brad and I in to see him as soon as possible on Tuesday. I was immensely grateful and at peace knowing that John had cared for Cale during his final preparation. With a quiet strength born of years of experience, John then stood with Brad and I as we gazed upon our son, a hand upon each of our backs. With this same quiet strength he advised us on the choice of a casket and helped us make other decisions that needed to be made.

Kevin, also, was incredible – kind, compassionate, understanding. He bent over backwards it seemed, to meet our needs. When we said we didn't want a traditional funeral, he said fine. When we said we wanted to play Cale's music during visiting hours, he said fine. When I said that might include some songs by Nine Inch Nails and Marilyn Manson, Kevin said "Cool"! Cale's favourite candies in a dish on the table – fine. Only one night of viewing – fine. No official religious service – fine. Nothing was out of the realm of possibility.

Others were there to help as well, with a variety of kind acts, which we could never imagine. My friend, and colleague Michelle Friesen, presented me with a moment of humour in the midst of chaos and sadness. Uncomfortable around large dogs, Michelle arrived at my house intent on vacuuming and washing my kitchen and dining room floors. While I offered a mop, she chose instead to scrub the floor on her hands and knees, which Chelsea thought was wonderful. The vision of my dog-fearing friend nose to nose with my large friend-loving dog was a wonderful piece of comic relief.

Food began showing up at our house in pots, pans, bags and coolers. Friends and family members called with offers of help. Upon hearing the news from Joanne, **Sam Burns, a friend and counselor I had been seeing for many years, cleared his calendar for Tuesday evening and spent hours listening and supporting Brad and I. He sent us home with a plate of cheese, crackers and Arrowroot cookies….encouraging us to eat the cookies, if nothing else. My hairdresser contacted me through Joanne to say she would be honoured to do my hair before Cale's funeral. Armed with all the pertinent information, Joanne contacted our life insurance broker to initiate the process of cashing in Cale's life insurance, which we would need to pay for the funeral. My mother took over plans and payment for the meal following the service. My brother, Norm, made arrangements to pick up Brad's truck from work, where it had been left, so we didn't have to worry about it. Hearing that I couldn't get the image of Cale's face from Monday night out of my head, my brother Gilles had one of Cale's grade eight graduation pictures blown up. Friends stopped by just to hug us and other friends called to say they had lit candles for our family and were praying for us. Emails began arriving from our friends and Cale's. The acts of kindness never seemed to end, and carried on long after the funeral had ended.

In the hours and days following Cale's death I found myself searching for signs that he was okay. I soon came to realize something I have carried with me ever since – if I am open, the signs are plentiful. I only have to believe.

Prior to Cale's death a very interesting situation had been taking place involving a beautiful bright red male cardinal. This stunning bird had been knocking at Cale's window every morning for weeks. He would throw himself at the window repeatedly. For Cale, an avid animal lover, the possibility of the cardinal harming himself was of great concern. However, Cale was also an avid lover of sleeping in past 6 a.m. and his gorgeous red-feathered friend was an early riser. Cale occasionally found himself becoming quite frustrated at the bird's antics.

The day Cale died, the cardinal stopped visiting his window. It has never again visited that window, or any other window in our home, although it is now rare for a day to go by without a cardinal visiting one of the trees in our yard.

The day after Cale died my friend, Leasa, a member of my Woman Within E Circle, a women's support group I belong to, called to ask if Brad and I would be open to attending a support circle that was being planned for us on Wednesday evening. Knowing the support I had received for this group in the past, I agreed. When Brad and I arrived more than 30 men and women were gathered to support us. The gathering included some people that we didn't know or had only met once or twice, who had heard about Cale and just wanted to support us in anyway possible.

The evening included a shamanic drumming and healing ceremony headed by **Barb Smith. She spoke of meditating in preparation for the evening, and said Cale had come to her in the form of a cardinal, and told her he was at peace and no longer suffering. I barely knew Barb at that time, and she knew nothing about Cale's cardinal visitor, so I was overwhelmed as she spoke. It was an incredible sign for me, and what I needed to hear. It was also only part of an incredible evening of support and healing.

The next day while running errands in preparation for the funeral, I looked for a cardinal figurine to bring to the funeral home. At one store after another I turned away in despair, unable to find anything related to cardinals.

Having given up on finding a cardinal figurine, I made one more stop at a drug store to buy a few bags of Campino's, one of Cale's favourite candies. I wanted to have a bowl of these candies at the funeral home. I checked the store shelves for a cardinal, certain there would be none, and I was right. However, while checking out, the cashier, a woman whose name tag read Betty, asked me if I had found everything I needed. It was the last straw. I broke down, quietly crying, and explained that my son had died, and why I just wanted a cardinal figurine for the funeral. Betty, whom I had never met before, grabbed my hand, saying "come with me."

As I followed her out of the store, she yelled back to another cashier to tell her she'd be right back. She pointed to her vehicle, and told me to follow her in mine. Betty led me to her house, where she ran inside, returning in a few moments with a beautiful figurine of two cardinals. She gave me a hug, told me to keep it, and said she had to get back to work. With the figurine in my hand, I drove about two blocks before having to pull off the road. I dissolved in a torrent of tears, overcome by the kindness of a stranger and another much needed sign that Cale was with me. That figurine took centre stage at the funeral, surrounded by the bowl of candy and photographs of Cale.

The signs continued to arrive over the coming days and months. A woman at whose home Cale had spent a great deal of time, arrived at the funeral home with a gift. Knowing nothing about the cardinal stories, she handed me a small stuffed cardinal. She explained that on each of his recent visits to her home, Cale had tried to sneak the stuffed bird out of her house. After his death, she felt he was meant to have it. Brad and I would later decide to place it in the container with Cale's urn. A few days after the funeral I was working on the computer and went to 'my internet favourites' to look something up. There, on top of the list, was the link to a short cut called 'Attracting Cardinals to Your Yard.' I had no idea how the link had gotten into my favourites folder, and as the days went by and I questioned others, no one else knew either.

Nothing could have prepared me for Cale's funeral and the outpouring of support and grief from our friends, family, neighbours and community. As overwhelming as this was, however…it was nothing compared to the teenagers who began showing up the moment the funeral home doors were opened. Cale's friends and fellow students began arriving, sometimes one by one, sometimes in groups, sometimes accompanied by parents and older siblings. They were devastated by the loss of their friend, scared and confused. They wanted to understand. They wanted everything to be normal. Along with the teenagers came teachers, principals, counselors and school support staff, as well as students, staff and parents from other schools Cale had attended. As Cale's music – a CD of songs picked by his brother Adam - played in the background, hundreds and hundreds of people turned out to pay their respects to my son. I would later learn that as the ceremony was held people stood filling all the halls and rooms of the funeral home and spilling out onto the streets and sidewalks.

Cale's friends and fellow students alternately warmed and broke my heart. Their grief and confusion was great; their disbelief even greater. Tiny girls and larger, strapping young men alike dissolved in my arms, their bodies shaking as they sobbed uncontrollably. I held them, trying to lessen their grief while in some way holding onto my son through them. In between tears and embraces Cale's friends shared with me their knowledge of Cale; little stories of classroom antics or kind deeds he had done; how his smile had lit up the hallway at school. I treasured each word, tucking them away in my heart like tiny, shining gems.

Over the next two days I alternated between disbelief and intense grief. At times I would see myself separated from the events taking place around me, as if watching from outside my body. Friends and family members would dissolve in tears, and I would wonder what I could do, or say, to help them.

Then reality would roar into the room like an angry lion, fangs dripping, nostrils flaring and eyes flashing. One glimpse of Cale's grandmother and grandfather and their quiet strength and dignity, or my mother, who was so well known in our community and surrounded by friends, brought me right back to reality. It was impossible for me not to accept the reality as I watched Adam – his anger and disbelief so obvious in his withdrawn state. Lost in my own despair and grief, I was terrified of losing Adam as well, to this tragedy. My heart ached to reach out to him, but I had no words…nothing I could say to make it right; to bring Cale back. The sadness was intensely visible on Ange's face, and the faces of Cale's cousins.

Despite her recent open heart surgery my sister did not leave my side. She and I had been through hell together in our lives and had always been there for each other. This would be no different. Somehow Joanne could sense those moments when my legs began to buckle, and grief washed over me…those moments when I was certain I could not go on. She would reach out her hand grasping mine tightly, and urge me to continue…for Cale and for his friends. Brad, too, did not leave my side, nor do I think that he could have. Panic would begin to set in the moment he moved even a few feet away. My life had been ripped from its foundation, and my son, an incredible blond haired black-eyed boy whom I had given birth to and had forged an incredible bond with, had been ripped from my arms and my life. Nothing was safe. I trusted nothing. I was overcome with a sense of dread and loss, certain that I would lose Brad, Adam, Ange, Joanne – everyone and everything I held dear. It would be a long, long time before this sense of panic, of impending loss, would begin to ease.

Unlike the day Cale died, the day of his funeral dawned bright, sunny and warm. Spring was in the air…and in my heart. As hard as the day would be, Brad and I were determined that it be a celebration of Cale's life. Despite my sadness and the pain in my heart, I also felt a sense of peace, knowing Cale would have been happy that we 'celebrated.'

Prior to the service Cale's CD played in the background. While Adam said little during the days following Cale's death, his choice of music for Cale's funeral CD spoke volumes. He had included a few songs at mine and his father's request. The rest of the songs he chose, and in the lyrics of each I heard the messages my wonderful, intelligent oldest son was giving to his brother. It was for me, confirmation of just how badly

19

Adam was hurting and missing Cale. He may have been helped in his endeavours by Ange, but I'm not sure and I have never asked. But the messages were clear in the songs that he chose – 'Everybody Needs a Little Time Away' by Chicago, Shine by Collective Soul, Knockin' on Heaven's Door by Guns n' Roses, No More Tears and Dreamer by Ozzy Osbourne – the later being one of Cale's favourite songs – and more. In the months following the funeral I would make copies of this CD for so many people – youth and adults alike – that I lost track.

Claire began Cale's service by welcoming our guests and by explaining our desire to celebrate Cale's life. It was the beginning of what truly was a beautiful and uniquely 'Cale' service. One of my very close friends, Peggy, sang Sarah McLaughlin's Angel and another song. As the haunting melody and guitar notes floated through the funeral home I could hear the sobs of guests behind and around me. I was grateful and humbled by her incredible gift. Later this incredible woman would organize a musical benefit to raise funds to help Brad and I get through the following months. Her amazing gift would allow us to take some time to decide what we wanted to do in terms of our eventual return to the work force.

My mother, Cale's grandmother, read a poem that I had written years ago – 'A Prayer to Jesus' for help and support during difficult times. It seemed fitting. Dave, a young musician friend of my niece Kari had taken a poem I had written after Cale's death and put it to music.

I am Cale
the son, brother, nephew, cousin and friend you have always known.
I am only a heartbeat away,
Open your eyes and you will recognize me
In that bright-eyed boy at the supermarket, all impish grins and swirling energy
In that young man full of mischief and volatile passion, sweetness and sensitivity, anger and frustration, hope and belief
Close your eyes and you will feel me
In the gentle breeze and blustery winds; the silent snowflakes and pelting rain
Open your heart and remember me

Not for what you have heard from others, but for what I have openly and gratefully shared with you – my humour, creativity, fears, joys, passion.

Remember me not for the judgments others made about me, but for the reality that you knew – the truth of who I was, what I loved, what I craved, what I gave, what I shared.

Hear me
> In the songs my mother sings
> The words my father speaks
> The dreams my brother dreams

Feel me in the tears and laughter, anger and joy of my friends.

Honour me
> For always reaching for my dreams
> For the risks I took, the beliefs I was willing to fight for
> The anger I invoked, the love I nurtured
> The hugs I craved and shared with others
> The love in my heart.

If you can't find me…just be
> Be silent
> Be open
> Be ready
> Be willing

Place your hand on your heart
I am there.

Dave sang the song with the kind music Cale would have loved. With his guitar screaming, the young man belted out the words of the song. I was aware of the fact that many people in the audience were uncomfortable with this form of music, and found myself smiling, knowing how happy it would have made Cale. In contrast, Ozzy's Dreamer, one of Cale's favourite songs, was played and later people would tell me they never knew Ozzy sang like that.

Claire opened up the service to members of the audience and one by one Cale's friends spoke of his influence on them through his life and death, and their sadness at losing him. One of his elementary school teachers spoke of his gifts, including his anger, and what these gifts had taught her. Friends promised, in his honour, not to hurt themselves, and to ask for help. One young man took a razor blade out of his wallet and placed it in Cale's pocket, promising never to attempt to hurt himself again.

The service ended with the performance of Eric Clapton's Tears in Heaven by Cale's long time friend Jason Cabanaw. A talented musician, Jason played guitar and sang the song that I had requested, marking the end of Cale's service.

Brad and I had made a decision to have Cale's body cremated, so we had not expected to have a funeral procession. However, the funeral home had been contacted by the high school the day before with a special request. Staff and students wanted a chance to honour Cale, and had requested a procession past the school. Brad and I agreed.

Following Jason's performance Cale's pallbearers – his cousins Jason, Shawn, Heath, Shane and Justin, and one friend Roger – carried his casket to the hearse. We followed as it made its way passed the high school. Time seemed to stand still as we approached the school where both sides of the road were lined with students, teachers and staff, more than 1,000 people. In the middle of the crowd stood Cale's friend Mike Hicks, wearing his kilt and full Scottish regalia, and playing Amazing Grace on the bagpipes. All around him students wiped tears from their eyes. In that moment as we passed Mike, what little that was left of my resolve crumbled. The pain in my heart was so monumental I felt I couldn't breath. It seemed so incredibly ironic to me that the love and acceptance that Cale had so badly desired in his life, was so obviously present in his death.

Chapter Three

About a month or so before Cale died, on a particularly calm winter day, Cale and I were laying on the trampoline, looking at the sky. It was something we did often because Cale smoked cigarettes and was not allowed to smoke in the house. Lying on our backs looking at the sky, Cale would smoke his cigarette and talk about whatever was on his mind. Usually Chelsea would race around the yard scaring up imaginary playmates and trying to entice us to join her antics. On this night, she jumped up on the trampoline and lay down on the other side of me.

Cale seemed lost in thought. When he did speak, his words caught me off guard and set off a spiral of panic in my chest. I fought to stay calm as we spoke.

"Mom, if anything happens to me, you'll keep fighting for kids like me, kids who are having trouble - right?" Cale asked.

"Cale, nothing's going to happen to you," I answered, alarmed. "Let's not even talk about it…we'll get through whatever comes up."

"Okay, but you'll keep helping kids, right?" he asked again.

I remember wanting to ignore him, or to get mad and tell him to stop talking like that. I remember wanting to tell him again that nothing was going to happen; that we could handle anything. Inside me, however, something was telling me Cale needed to hear my answer; needed to hear that I would continue to advocate through my work and volunteer positions, for changes to the children's mental health care system, and to reach out to other youth in crisis.

Taking a deep breath, I told him what he wanted to hear, and what he already knew. "Yes, Cale, I will keep fighting; I will always fight to help kids."

I felt something in me die as Cale let out a huge sigh. I knew something had changed. I didn't know what, or how, but my mother's soul...the ancient wisdom that every mother carries, knew.

"I love you mom," Cale said.

"I love you too, Cale," I responded, with silent tears running from the corners of my eyes. It was the last time that I remember Cale saying these words before he died. Little did I know how much I would come to treasure them.

We lay quietly, mother and son, side by side, looking at the stars, until we became too cold to stay outside any longer.

It was easy for me to put these words out of my mind in the coming weeks, as Cale showed signs of improvement on the Lithium. A day or two after his death, however, they came back in full force during the course of a phone conversation with a friend, Susan Hess.

Susan was, and remains, president of Parents for Children's Mental Health, a provincial organization. She was in Toronto at the time of Cale's death. She had developed the idea for the Quilt of Honour Campaign. The Quilt of Honour was a testament to the many children who have mental health problems – real, painful and sometimes severe problems. When Susan began envisioning the quilt she wanted it to reflect the fact that at any given time, one in five children suffers from a mental health issue, and one in 10 children seriously considers suicide. She was creating the Quilt of Honour to honour all children with mental illness, those who are alive and those who have died.

The quilt had been partially completed months earlier when Susan had contacted me to ask if Cale's name could be added to the quilt. I was dedicated to increasing awareness about children's mental health and amazed at the quilt and in awe of Susan's work and her dedication. But I declined. Cale has been the centre of attention in a negative way for so many years because of his illness. I just wanted to give him a chance to be a 'normal' teenager...to not have to be a 'kid with a problem.' Susan had understood my decision at that time.

When I talked to Susan following Cale death, everything had changed. The quilt was nearing completion. I wanted everyone to know what had happened, and why. I wanted everyone to know that children and teenagers do suffer from mental illness, and what can happen if we as a society don't pay attention. I wanted everyone to know that we would keep losing our children to suicide or violence or drugs or other addictions, if families couldn't access the proper treatment for mental illness. I just wanted everyone to know.

As a result of that conversation with Susan a spot was reserved for Cale on the Quilt of Honour. The quilt was unveiled at the Children's Mental Health Ontario conference in May of 2003, and made its Windsor debut at a local children's health care centre in August. I couldn't bring myself to attend. It was too soon.

But the next spring I traveled to Chatham to view the quilt for the first time, and hear Susan speak. The beautiful white and red quilt hung from a stand at the front of the room. Susan's inspiration for the quilt had been the old-fashioned paper doll chains. The quilt is divided into blocks, each adorned with five paper doll figures. At the bottom of many of the individual blocks is the name of a child with mental health problems. As Susan talked I learned that the red and white figures that are depicted holding hands represent children who have received help for their mental health problems.

The figures standing alone in the paper doll chain, not connected with the other four dolls, represent children who are waiting for help. The blocks with totally white figures represent children who have taken their own lives. In total, nine courageous children and their families were, at that time, represented on the quilt.

As I listened to Susan and looked at the quilt, my eyes were drawn to the bottom right hand block. There, in bright red, was my son's name. Above it, in white, was the figure representing him and his death. Beside Cale's block was the name of my friend's daughter, who was receiving assistance for her mental health difficulties. I was comforted knowing the two were side by side.

Wanting nothing more than to get up and run my hand over his name and the quilt, I forced myself instead to listen as Susan spoke.

One of the biggest challenges facing children with mental illness and their families, Susan said, is the shame and stigma of mental health problems. Fear of stigma and the resulting discrimination discourages people from getting the help they need.

Susan then shared a story of having been in Peterborough, Ontario recently with the quilt. Following her presentation three teenagers came up to talk to her. They had known Cale and were horrified and saddened by his death. They had met him a few years earlier when his Grade 8 class spent a week at Muskoka Woods. They remembered him as funny and smart. Susan wanted me to know this, and that she felt Cale's presence often as she traveled the province and country with the quilt. I was overwhelmed, and thankful that the quilt was making a difference.

I did get to touch the quilt that day. In fact, I sat on the floor with Cale's 'block' in my lap, running my fingers over the letters of his name, tears flowing freely from my eyes. It was a difficult situation, and a definitive one – more proof that Cale truly was gone. It was also very healing and provided me with more evidence of just how many people Cale had affected during his short life. This, I realized, was one of the many gifts Cale brought me through his death.

In the weeks and months that followed Cale's death I lived my life in a sort of shock. Early on I made a promise to celebrate Cale and look for the gifts in his life and death, rather than choosing to remain in constant mourning. It was a decision I had to renew on a daily basis, and it was not easy. There were many days I forgot the decision, or didn't know how to keep the promise, and many times I simply couldn't find the gifts. I missed my son so incredibly much that I couldn't breath. My chest would constrict with pain so bad I feared I was having a heart attack. I knew there were many gifts, and I knew that when I was open to them, they appeared. But sometimes choosing to be open was more than I could bear and took more energy than I had….it just hurt too much.

During Cale's life, one of the greatest gifts he had ever given me was his willingness to talk to me. This gift took on even greater significance after his death. Cale and I were very close and had shared an incredible bond. Early in his life, when he felt nobody understood him, including other members of his family, he began talking to me. He had always told me what was happening with him; how he was feeling; what he was thinking. During his times of deep depression he described his thoughts of blackness and not wanting to live; of feeling like he could never please his father or others in his life; of feeling worthless and undeserving. During his manic highs, he described the feelings of high anxiety and being unable to slow down; of feeling stupid because of his impulsivity and the decisions he made which he felt were wrong. He spoke to me of his deep desire to please people, mostly his father and brother; and his overwhelming feelings of failure and inadequacy because, in his judgment, he was falling far short of this goal. Despite his tough-seeming exterior he was very sensitive and compassionate. He explained what happened when he became enraged or frustrated; how the control seemed to slip from his grasp and he could not stop himself. He described the fear he felt when his rage was out of control, and he couldn't seem to stop it. He described to me in detail the voices he heard, and his strong desire, at times, to die. He told me of his fear that the voices would never go away, that he would always be 'different'. He told me of his desire to be accepted and loved, and his unwillingness to believe that he was. He told me how tired he was of fighting himself, and the world, all the time.

The value of Cale's gift to me in sharing these words was, and remains, almost indescribable. When Cale died I felt no guilt - grief, disbelief, sorrow, despair, horror - but no guilt. Because of Cale's words, I was able to understand why he had made the choice he had. I wouldn't realize how great this gift truly was until months later when I joined a support group. There I would learn that guilt is often one of the key emotions left behind for survivors of suicide, and the hardest to work through.

Brad and I talked a lot, and we were blessed with an incredible support network or friends and family who were available in a moment if we needed them. Leasa organized a phone and card tree which resulted in friends phoning to check in and sending cards with words of support for six months following Cale's death! On a daily basis I opened cards, many adorned with cardinals, from numerous friends, with messages of hope, inspiration and the spiritual energy I craved. Just as often I answered the phone to find a friend calling just to check in and see how things were going. Peggy, who had sang at the funeral, organized a benefit concert to raise money for Brad and I, to allow us to take some extra time off work following the funeral.

In the weeks and months to come I used every opportunity to talk about Cale and children's mental health. While I was passionate about the cause before Cale's death; afterwards it became a crusade. I took on the three-foot rule – if you were within three feet of me, you heard the script. I agreed to two separate interviews with the Windsor Star which lead to articles on the subject. A few months after Cale's death I was invited to address a meeting of service providers, Windsor city politicians and others interested in children's mental health. I was given three minutes to tell my story. So I began writing. I figured I would make the very best use of the three minutes. I remember preparing the story, and thinking I no longer had anything to loose. I had lost my son. I might as well lay it on the line.

When I arrived at city hall to attend the meeting, I didn't care who was there, or why. I just wanted them to feel my pain in the hopes that it might bring change. And so I spoke.

Cale is an incredible young man. He is 16-years-old and quite handsome – blond hair and dark brown eyes. He is intelligent and funny, creative, sensitive and compassionate, angry and volatile. He's a great talker and loves to talk to me about everything…to the point where I've often I felt like I had received a little too much information. Cale is an incredible friend to me as well as being my son.

Cale is dead.

At about 8:30 p.m. on April 7 I opened the bathroom door and was greeted by the image of my son, hanging from the top of our shower, his face blue and swollen, an electrical extension cord embedded in his neck. It is an image that burned itself in my brain and heart in the ensuing moments as I struggled to cut him down, call 9-1-1 and perform CPR and mouth to mouth resuscitation, even though I knew it was too late. It is an image that will remain with me every moment of every day for the rest of my life.

"Cale chose to end his life that evening. He chose death over the intense struggle he had been waging for years and years against bipolar disease and anxiety disorders. He chose death over the constant struggle to fit into a world which always seemed to be just outside of his grasp. He chose death over medical and social service systems which are stretched to the max, and could not help him unless he was in the depths of crisis...and then could only offer band aids. He chose death over an education system, which, through most of his 13 years of school, viewed him as a behavioural problem rather than looking beyond his symptoms to the incredible burden of mental illness this beautiful young man carried.

He chose death by his own hand because we, the society in which he lived – failed him.

It's kind of funny in a way, because I've always considered our family to be one of the luckier families of children with mental health challenges. He had a mother who refused to be quiet and stop fighting for help. Cale was able to access some services and had the help of a pediatrician who believed in him, and in my husband and I as parents. She wanted nothing more than to help. But her hands were tied to a great extent as well, by a system with too little money, too few child psychiatrists, a government which doesn't seem to care enough and too little time and resources to help the remaining 800 children who are waiting for mental health services. The saddest part of this is that we have wonderful services right here in our community, but families can't access them unless they are in crisis – not just the edge of crisis, but drowning in the depths of the well.

I miss my son every moment of every day, and will miss him every moment of every day for the rest of my life; my heart aches to see his smile, hear his laugh, lay on the trampoline staring at the black sky with him while we talk about life. His loss grabs me with a vengeance when I am least expecting it, and my heart constricts. The pain is unbearably severe….it leaves me wondering if I've suffered a heart attack. I know now that hearts really do break!

But I will never, ever question whether or not I did everything I could for my son. I know my family tried every avenue possible to us to try to access the help he needed, even when it seemed like every door in this province was closed.

There are many people in this province, in this government, who need to take a close look at what is happening in the children's mental health sector. These people need to ask themselves if they are doing everything they can.

Would it make a difference if it were not my son who lay in the casket on April 10 and 11 – but the child of one of the decision makers in our government? Would changes come then? Would they come faster? Don't misunderstand me…it is not my desire, nor my wish that anyone else lose a child to suicide. I just wonder what needs to happen to bring about the change needed.

I cannot have my son back. No matter how much I cry, rant and rave, plead and beg, pray and bargain….Cale is dead. How many more children from our municipality of Windsor and Essex County have to join Cale before changes are made? How many more children and families are we willing to sacrifice to a system which does not provide children with proper and adequate mental health services?

How many more Cales will there be?

If the answer to this is even one…shame on us all.

I can't remember everyone who was sitting around the mayor's table that day, but I do remember that most had tears in their eyes when I finished. I remember Amber, who, being the incredible friend she was had offered to come with me, clutching my hand tightly. I remember fighting back what felt like a torrent of tears welling up in my chest. I don't remember leaving the meeting or driving home. I remember being exhausted.

Chapter Four

Brad and I had initially thought about placing Cale's ashes with his cousin Cory, my sister Joanne's first child, who had died of leukemia in February 1986. Cale was conceived within an hour of the time Cory died, so although they never met, I had always felt they were connected. However, as the days passed I became quite distraught about the thought of Cale being in a cemetery. I hated cemeteries and always had. I found no peace in them. I never had. I hated the thought of having to go to a cemetery to visit Cale.

One day when Brad and I were discussing options it dawned on us that we wanted Cale out near our pond. Brad, Cale, Adam and some of their friends had dug and built the pond a few years earlier. Located in the northeast corner of our yard, it is big and has a beautiful waterfall. We had purposely made the area look natural, with driftwood and rocks, rather than manicured and 'gardened.'

Brad and I purchased a cement planter with a top to place by the pond. On a sunny day a month or so after Cale's death John and Judy visited our house, John carrying with him Cale's urn. John had been lovingly protecting and caring for the urn in the days since Cale's death, waiting for our decision. This day would be the only occasion when I would witness John's silent strength and solid support crumble. He and Judy helped us place Cale's urn in the planter, along with the stuffed cardinal and some other items from friends and family. John then placed a loonie in the planter. Cale had always borrowed loonies and toonies from people to buy coffee. The loonie hit the bottom of the planter, and John began to cry. Holding tight to each other John, Judy, Brad and I cried as we welcomed Cale to his new home. It was then that I truly realized how very difficult Cale's death had been on John, who had been such a solid rock for us during the funeral preparations.

Brad and I left the planter open for a few weeks to allow friends and family to place items in. Among the items was a letter from Cale's Godfather whom we had not spoken to for close to fifteen years, and pictures of Cale and his friends. When we felt enough time had passed Brad sealed the top of the planter to keep the moisture from entering. From the moment the decision was made to place the planter by the pond, I felt at peace, knowing I could visit and talk to Cale anytime I wish.

A short time later Brad's family – Brenda, Keith, Jason, Amanda, Kristy, Shawn, Judy and John and his parents arrived at our house with a beautiful wrought iron garden set. The set contained two benches and a table which we placed out by the pond. The gift completed what has now become a peaceful haven where our family and friends and Cale's friends can visit him.

Not too long after the funeral I decided to get a tattoo for Cale, since he had not been able to. Friends and family members found this amusing as I had always swore I would never get a tattoo. Somewhat nervous I made arrangements with a tattoo artist at a Windsor tattoo parlour. After a process which lasted a few hours and hurt more than some people had reported, and less than others, I left the store with a beautiful red cardinal in a dream catcher adorning my right shoulder blade. Cale's name was tattooed above the dream catcher. A few months later I would return for a mirror image on my left shoulder blade, this one with Adam's name and a wolf. They are constant reminders for me of the two greatest gifts I have ever received.

Pictures were a constant reminder of Cale and I sought them out regularly. Right after the funeral I put his pictures up everywhere throughout the house. I desperately needed to see his face. A large poster with a picture of him in the centre was displayed in the dining room. It had been signed by many of the people who attended his funeral, and I often stopped to read the messages. The handwritten messages were a reminder to me that Cale had been loved and cherished as a friend and human being.

"Remember you always."

"Make room in heaven, Cale's moving in!"

"Miss your smiling face."

"Thanks for the memories and for playing house with me when no one else would. Love you forever."

"It won't be the same."

"I'll always be hoping for your guidance. Look out for me bud."

"Not here, but not forgotten."

"We will miss your laughter."

"You are always in my heart."

"It can't hurt much to die if it hurts so much more to stay alive – from those of us who know your pain."

"I'll always remember you and the crazy bus rides."

"I'm sorry Cale. I should have stood up for you man."

For months it seemed that every time I walked passed this picture I found a new message that I hadn't noticed before, or had read and forgotten. This picture became a source of comfort for me, and a symbol of just how much Cale was loved and how badly he was missed.

With the help of friends we cleaned Cale's room out immediately after his death. It was just too hard for me to see the chaotic mess that had been Cale's domain and not feel as if my heart was being ripped out of my chest. Every time I looked into the room I remembered my last visit to his room, and the last words he spoke to me. When I passed the doorway, I remembered the arguments with Cale over the state of the room, and begging him to at least clear a path through the clothes, books, wrappers, packages, CDs, and other odds and ends on the floor so that he could escape in the event of a fire.

"It's fine, mom," he would say. "It's my room."

No amount of begging or pleading could convince him to clean it, although the occasional bribe was successful. What did work, sometimes, were my offers to work with him to clean his room. On those occasions we would work side by side creating from the chaos some semblance of order and talking about everything under the sun as we worked. How I missed those conversations as I began to work on his room following his death. However, as much as I needed his room cleared out, I wasn't ready to go through his things. They were put into plastic tote boxes and stored. I would take them out one at a time over the coming months to sort through his things, pack away the items I wanted to keep and give away items of significance to family members and friends.

Everyday life was the hardest. That may sound funny, but that's the way it was. I expected to be overcome with sadness on Mother's Day. I expected to feel my heart constrict when I talked to Brad, Adam or Ange about Cale. I expected to be sad and to miss seeing him in the house or sitting on the back step having a cigarette, or hearing him on the phone. I expected to cry when I pictured his smile. Cale's entire face had lit up when he laughed – a true, deep, belly laugh. I even expected to feel a bittersweet emptiness whenever I saw a cardinal.

What I didn't expect – and what brought me to my knees over and over again – were the little things that I would not have thought of in a million years.

Cale, Adam and Agne had always preferred Pepsi over Coke, which was my favourite. Cale had been quite vocal about this preference and often teased me when we were in a store buying pop. Usually he managed to convince me to buy Pepsi instead.

One day shortly after the funeral I attempted to go grocery shopping... a fairly innocuous activity, or so I imagined. I decided to go to Wal Mart as opposed to a grocery store. Little did I realize this activity was wrought with emotional land mines, ready to explode under even the slightest pressure. Adam was staying with Ange and Cale was gone, so the need for groceries – both type and quantity - in our home had changed. One after another I picked up items which I normally would have bought for Cale or Adam, and placed them back on the shelf. My cart was about half full when I reached the pop aisle. Rounding the corner I ended up directly in front of a Pepsi display in the centre of the aisle. I wanted so badly to buy a case of Pepsi, yet I knew that without Cale, Adam or Ange at home, it would just sit in the fridge. As clear as day I heard the words "Coke sucks!" in my youngest son's voice. In that moment the realization that I had lost my youngest son to death struck me with the force of a freight train.

Feeling my knees buckle I grabbed the edge of the shopping cart and fell to ground where I began to sob. Somewhere in the back of my mind I heard a voice telling me to stop, that there were people watching. It didn't matter, and I couldn't stop.

Sobs rose up from the very pit of my stomach – primal, guttural, maternal howls which tore at my chest while forcing their way out of my throat. Somehow I found the strength to get up and run from the store. Sitting in my car, I continued weeping hysterically for what seemed like hours, and howled with grief and rage until my throat burned. I vowed never to go grocery shopping again, and in that moment, I believed I would not.

For months I fought terrifying panic attacks in which my heart felt as though it would jump out of my chest. They hit in stores or malls, the post office, bank and every time I tried to go to the gym to workout – anywhere there was likely to be people I did not know. They hit when I was driving, and would see a young man walking down the road dressed in black jeans and black t-shirt, with chains on his neck and in his belt loop, and blond hair on his head – or black or no hair, as Cale had tried them all. More than once I stopped my car, certain it was Cale, only to find myself staring at, and sometimes talking to, a complete stranger.

The panic attacks would hit, and my heart would start to hammer in my chest. I would break out in a cold sweat, yet feel like I was on fire. Unable to breath, I would be overcome with an intense feeling of dread, which would drop like a heavy woolen blanket over my head. Each time

Diane Simon

it would take all of my energy to get out of the building and back to my car, or if I was in my car, to pull over so I could call Brad on the cell phone, listening to his voice until the panic passed.

I couldn't stand not knowing where Brad, Adam and Ange were at all times. Ange was a like a daughter to me, and I was certain something bad would happen to her, my son or my husband. Moment by moment, every day, I worried, panicking if I hadn't heard from them. The fact that Adam was living at Ange's house made it more difficult for me. I had no way of knowing where they were or if they were okay. Logically I knew I couldn't expect to keep track of their every movement. My heart, however, was not operating on logic.

I decided to buy Mike cell phones for the four of us, which definitely provided me with a modicum of peace. I still worried, but knew that if I needed to, I could contact them at any time.

I remember being in Windsor one day and being unable to get ahold of Brad. For some reason we were unable to connect by regular or cell phone, although I can't remember why. I drove home, trying not to panic and speed, with this conversation going on in my head – logic versus emotion. Something must be wrong versus his cell phone battery is dead. He must be hurt versus he is outside working in the yard and can't hear the phone. Back and forth, back and forth the conversation went for 45 minutes.

As I pulled into the driveway I noticed the exhaust tube exiting the hole in the large door of my husband's shop. With dread I approached the garage door only to find it locked. My broken heart and tortured mind immediately assumed my husband had chosen to join our son. I collapsed on the ground, begging God not to let this happen because I couldn't go through this again. This is how Brad found me a few minutes later. He hadn't known the door was locked, and had been fixing the exhaust on a car, hence the hose. He was devastated by the pain in my face. I think that was the point where I, and he, realized how very fearful I was of losing him and Adam.

Often the panic attacks hit when they seemed to make little sense. On the day I was scheduled to return to work I drove round and round the block, unable to pull into the parking lot. Finally, tears streaming down my face, I turned my car towards home. I decided not to return to work.

I had been employed on a contract basis, so it wasn't really difficult to work out. Brad, however, had been working for TST Overland for seven years on straight afternoons. He had also been running his own business part time, specializing in antiques, street rods, customizations and general repairs. While the latter was his passion, he had not been ready to make the leap to full time self employed business owner.

After Cale died Brad attempted to go back to work, but lasted only a few days. It was just too difficult, and there were too many memories. The night Cale died Brad had been sitting in the lunch room, reading a book called The Bipolar Child, by Dr. Demitri Papalos and his wife Janice. In the few years before his death Brad had been working very hard to understand Cale's illness and build a better relationship with him. The book, which I had purchased and found incredibly helpful, was providing some answers for Brad that evening. But Brad also had many questions, especially after my numerous calls earlier that evening. When Officer James arrived, Brad knew immediately that something was terribly wrong.

So, returning to work, Brad was ambushed by the memories which lurked behind the door of the lunchroom. As well, with only one other person on his shift, someone whom Brad had little contact or interaction with, Brad found himself way too alone with his thoughts and no one to talk to. Adding to his stress and emotional unease, Brad worried about being at work and knowing I was home alone, much like the evening Cale died. Prior to Cale's death, with Brad working the afternoon shift and Adam with Ange, I usually spent my evenings alone with Cale. Even if Adam had been home, Brad knew I was trying not to talk to him about his brother's death. It was obvious, the few times I had tried, that Adam was visibly uncomfortable and not ready to talk. I didn't want to push him. For Brad, though, it was one more reason to worry about me being home by myself in the evening.

Brad decided to take a leave of absence from work and made plans to go full time with his business. It was a decision I had wanted for Brad for some time, and the boys had also desired. Cale in particular had been very vocal about his desire for Brad to leave TST, and in recent months had enjoyed spending time working on projects in the garage with Brad. I chose to look upon this as another gift from Cale through his death – a catalyst for change for Brad.

I spent much of my time in the coming months reading everything I could find that pertained to suicide, bipolar disorder, mental illness in children, teens and adults, depression and schizophnrenia. I raged and bullied my way through books like *Grieving Mental Illness* by Virginia Lafond; *The Bipolar Disorder Survival Guide* by David Milkowitz; *he Last Taboo* by Scott Simmie, *Night Falls Fast – Understanding Suicide,* and *An Unquiet Mind* by Kay Redfield Jamison; *Acquainted With the Night – A Father's Story* by Paul Raeburn; *The Suicide of My Son – A Story of Childhood Depression* by Trudy Carlson; *Andrew, You Died Too Soon* by Corinne Chilston; *Suicide, the Forever Decision* by Paul G. Quinnett; *Living When A Loved One Has Died* by Earl A. Grollman; *When Life Hurts* by Phillip Yancy; *When the Bough Breaks – Forever After the Death of a Son or Daughter* by Judith Bernstein; *Sanity and Grace – A Journey of Suicide, Survival and Grace* by Judy Collins; *Mental Illness for Women* by Rita Baron Faust; and *My Son, My Son – A Guide to Healing After Death, Loss, Suicide* by Iris Bolton. I was determined, as I opened each one, to find the information I needed to help me understand and cope with the trauma of my son's death. They all helped in some way, shape or form.

Spring came and went that year, and somehow I missed it. I would look back later and be unable to recall the grass turning green or the buds and leaves springing to life on the bushes and trees. Normally one of my favourite times of year, the spring of 2003 could not penetrate the pain and numbness of my mind and this heavy, black, suffocating shroud had descended upon me.

I do, however, remember planning for a trip to a cottage just outside Algonquin Park that August. Adam and Ange were coming with us, and I couldn't wait to get away and just be with my family. I wanted some healing time with Adam, who had closed down and wouldn't talk about his brother, and Ange, who was grieving so deeply. I knew how difficult it was at times to live with Cale. I knew first hand the anger and frustration that could erupt within me, even though I understood his mental illness, at his 'behaviours' and his stubbornness, rage and obstinance. However, despite the conflict and turmoil that sometimes was life with Cale, I knew that Adam had loved his brother, and was hurting at a deep, deep level that I couldn't seem to reach. I also knew that Ange, who had loved Cale like a sister, was hurting as well. Recently I had come upon Ange sitting on my couch looking very forlorn and had asked her what was wrong.

"I'll never be an aunt," she had replied, her beautiful blue eyes welling with tears.

In other words, Cale was gone. I didn't know what to say to this beautiful young woman who had stolen my heart. So I didn't speak. I hugged her close and we both cried.

So, when the opportunity to go to Algonquin arose, I desperately wanted some healing time with my family. I counted down the days until we left.

The night before we left Brad and I attended the 35th wedding anniversary of our friends Joe and Amber Porter. I was honoured to be invited, and to be a part of this special day, yet most of the evening passed in a fog. In the months to come I would come to realize how many blocks of time I had lost following Cale's death. Friends and family members would remind me of things I had said and done, but I had no memory of them. I suppose it was my mind's way of protecting me, of lifting the fog of shock slowly, carefully and only when I could handle it. Joe and Amber's anniversary was one of those evenings. I remember how beautiful the room looked as I entered and how happy Joe and Amber were. I remember sitting at a table with friends.

But I couldn't tell you what Amber wore or what we ate. I knew the pastor performing the vow renewal ceremony would be in Algonquin the next day to perform the marriage of my friend Peggy, to John Barwise, another friend. But I don't remember any of the words said by her or Joe and Amber during the ceremony.

I remember breathing a sigh of relief when we headed to Algonquin. I wasn't trying to get away from anyone...we had received such great support from family and friends. But I was so tired of pretending I was doing fine. I craved the opportunity to get away, to be near nature, to be with Brad, Adam and Ange.

Our vacation started with at Algonquin Park with Peggy and John's wedding, a wonderful event despite massive rains which threatened to postpone it. Our vacation at Red Deer Campground just outside Algonquin Park was bittersweet. I missed Cale incredibly, more than ever because he had loved camping and fishing and being up north. I knew how very much he would have loved being at Red Deer. I spent a lot of time looking out over the water and wondering if the pain would ever go away; if time would lessen the ache. I had little faith in the saying "time heals all wounds" but I did believe it might begin to hurt differently.

While missing Cale horribly, the vacation also offered Brad, Adam, Ange and I some badly needed healing time together. Along with Chelsea we ate and drank when we chose, swam, walked, played cards, shopped (Ange and I) and napped to our hearts delight, talked, laughed, cried and enjoyed our time together. I returned home refreshed, lighter and ready to carry on.

Throughout the summer, fall and into the coming year Cale's friends played an important part in my healing. They also played an important part in my ongoing education about children, youth and mental illness. Beginning with the funeral friends and other youth who struggled with mental illness reached out to us to let us know Cale was not alone; that they understood. One of his best friends, a young lady named **Laurie, visited me regularly and talked to me often about her friendship with Cale and her struggle with depression and attempted suicide. **Jordan Barker wanted Cale, wherever he was, to know he had not struggled alone. His delivered his message to us in a letter which he presented to me at the funeral.

"I can't say that I understand what you are going through. I cannot, in any way, say that I have been through what you must be dealing with. However, I suffer from manic-depression, and have recently been hospitalized for suicide attempts, and I know the feelings that Cale has been dealing with....

His memory will serve as a reminder that life is precious. If you ever feel that your son suffered alone, please be reminded that we all bleed the same way. There are others of us out there. I will keep Cale and your family in my thoughts and prayers. He many not be here anymore, but he will never be forgotten."

Listening to their stories I became more determined than ever to find out why children and youth were not being listened to and helped as they struggled with mental illness. I was also determined to find out why it seemed that society was not making the connection between mentally ill children growing up to be mentally ill adults.

Chapter Five

As determined as I was, however, I was constantly knocked backwards by emotions and memories. Often it was Cale's friends who helped me stand up again. On more than one occasion they provided the divine intervention that I desperately needed to continue living when I reached the point of simply not wishing to be present in this life anymore.

As the six month anniversary of Cale's death approached, I struggled with deep, deep sadness. I had watched as students headed back to school for what would have been Cale's last year in high school. Happy for his friends, I nonetheless couldn't help but realize that this was one of many events I would not watch my son participate in. His last year of school, graduation, college or university, marriage, children, a job…. all of these life events would not be.

Brad was invited to join some friends on a one week trip to Atlanta, Georgia, which would include attending a NASCAR race. I was happy for Brad, a huge NASCAR fan, and thought the trip would be good for him. I also felt certain I would be okay on my own for the six-month anniversary. I had plenty of friends and family to reach out to if needed. I encouraged Brad to go.

I had no idea how hard the sadness would hit me on night before the six month anniversary. I was overcome with grief and could not even summon the energy to call Adam, Ange, Joanne or a friend. Worse, I just didn't care. I curled up in my bed. Chelsea beside me, and sobbed for hours. The phone rang downstairs, and I ignored it. Chelsea whimpered and nudged my face, obviously sensing something horribly wrong, and I ignored her. I couldn't read, I couldn't think….and I didn't want to feel anymore. I begged for the pain, sadness and never-ending heartache to stop, telling God I just couldn't do it anymore.

When I was exhausted from crying and didn't have the energy to sob anymore, I just lay in bed, awake, for the rest of the night. I just didn't care anymore.

As dawn broke and light began to filter in through the bedroom window, I began to wonder how I could end my life. Curled up in bed, I struggled to find the energy to figure out how to kill myself. But I couldn't move from the bed. I was exhausted and thinking hurt. I wanted to end my life, but I didn't know how. I just didn't want to BE anymore.

Again, I started sobbing, begging God for help. If I was supposed to live, I needed help, I told Him. I couldn't carry on with this pain and longing. I couldn't carry on missing Cale so very, very much and hurting so very badly. I begged God for some kind of sign to help me figure out what I was supposed to do. I begged God to let me die.

And then the phone rang. Sitting on the nightstand beside my bed, where it had not been the night before, my cordless phone rang – piercing through the quiet like headlights on a moonless night. Too busy trying to figure out how the phone had gotten there, I forgot not to answer.

It was Robyn, Kelly's mom calling to ask if Kelly, Mike and some of Cale's friends could visit the next evening. The kids, Robyn said, had a gift for me they wanted, and needed, to deliver in person. I said yes and hung up the phone, realizing no matter how badly I wanted to die, I needed to be there for Cale's friends.

The next day Robyn, Kelly, Mike and his girlfriend Laura arrived at my house with a copy of their 2003 Phoebus – Leamington District Secondary School's high school yearbook. The last page of the book had been dedicated as a memorial to Cale. Pictures, poems and information about Cale covered the page. The book had been signed by students and teachers at the school. Again, at a time I desperately needed it, Cale's friends had reminded me of how many lives he had touched. More importantly, they had given me a new reason to live.

The next month Kelly, Mike and Laura, along with many of Cale's friends and members of our family, came to our home to celebrate Cale's 17th birthday. It had been raining most of the day, and stopped in early evening. With Ozzy Osbourne blaring from my nephew's car stereo, we gathered in a circle and sang Dreamer and Happy Birthday before releasing 20 white helium balloons into the night sky. A friend, Marg Stiers, who arrived just before we released the balloons, spoke of what appeared to be fireworks over our home as she was approaching. Looking out into the cloudy, foggy night we simply held each other close, knowing there was no explanation for the 'fireworks', and none was needed.

Christmas followed shortly afterwards, and I wanted no part of it. I knew that I should try, for Adam and Ange's sake, but I just didn't care. Cale had been the one who used to push me to put up decorations and a few years prior he, Adam and I had started a tradition of buying small potted trees which could then be planted in the yard, rather than cutting down trees. With Adam at Ange's house, and Cale gone, I just didn't care about Christmas. Brad and I ran away, heading to a hotel for the night. I brought my crock pot, threw in a roast and we were joined by Peggy and John for supper. No one spoke of Christmas, and it was easy to pretend we were just enjoying a night away. Brad's birthday followed in early January, and it was celebrated quietly and without fanfare.

Since Cale's death, I had lived with constant back pain and in early February 2004 I again underwent back surgery, this time to repair the damage we believed I had caused the night Cale died. My surgeon had warned me that he would likely need to insert rods and screws to support and strengthen my lower spine at the site of the first spinal fusion. Following surgery I learned the initial fusion had not been damaged as we had feared, and had actually healed well. Instead I had injured the two disks above the surgery site, and the nerve was compressed by scar tissue. Fusion and decompression surgery was performed, but no rods or screws were required.

About five months after Cale's death I finally contacted the Canadian Mental Health Association (CMHA) in Windsor-Essex for help in coping with the grief and pain. I had reached a point where I felt I was not making a great deal of headway, and I needed help. Deep, deep down, in the very core of my being, I ached with pain and longing I could not describe. Somehow I understood I was dying inside, dying as sure as my son had died. Somewhere inside, I knew that I needed help; that my very life depended on it. I had spiraled into this deep abyss of depression, and I didn't know how to crawl out of it by myself. Brad, too, was struggling in his own way.

It was a difficult phone call to make. I had turned to CMHA for help for Cale during his young life but CMHA is not mandated to assist children under 16. In fact, children's mental health services are not mandated under the health act. So my frustration level was high, and at the time that I was seeking help from CMHA it was just one more agency, one more organization who turned Cale away; one more agency who, I judged, had closed the door or turned its back.

So calling CMHA was a last resort, and a strong indication of just how badly I needed help. This call would literally save my life. In another one of God's gifts, my call was put through to the wrong person, but someone I was acquainted with. Glad that I wasn't talking to a stranger, and not realizing she did not cover the bereavement program for suicide survivors, I left a message. I told **Denise how vulnerable I felt having to call CMHA; how angry I was; and how desperately Brad and I needed help. I will never forget my surprise when Denise called me back, saying she understood my anger and vulnerability; and honoured my decision to reach out for help despite my anger. She couldn't explain why my phone call had been put through to her however she personally contacted bereavement counselor Christine MacMillan, who handled support for suicide survivors. Within days Brad and I were sitting in Christine's office talking. Soft spoken and gentle, Christine listened to our story, acknowledging my anger and courage at reaching out, and voicing her admiration for the work we had already done in the healing process. Christine honoured our courage, and admired how well we were coping, confirming that everything we were experiencing was normal. She acknowledged that past personal growth work we had undertaken was, and would continue, to assist us on our healing journey. I was surprised by her words, and felt welcome and safe.

Through Christine we joined the suicide survivors support group – a group of parents, brothers, sisters, spouses and friends of people who had completed suicide. It was here, in this board room surrounded by a group of strangers on the very first night that I truly, truly began to heal. This group, which met and continues to meet twice a month, quickly became one of my main lifelines. It was to this room, to this group of people that I could, and would, come repeatedly with all of my sadness, anger, disbelief, advice, grief, frustration…all of my reality. There was no judgment in the faces of the people who sat around the table. There was no disbelief in their voices or shaming in their words. The one thing we each shared was the loss of a loved one to suicide. It turned out to be one of only two places where I could be totally truthful and open, and knew I would be understood. The other was my E Circle meetings.

During the support group meetings at CMHA we often talked about the first year after a death. The common belief I was told was the first year would be worse. Friends and family members seemed to have this belief as well, often saying things like "the first year is almost over" or "his first birthday is gone" or "we made it through the first Christmas." I found myself agreeing. I approached the first anniversary of Cale's death, April 7, 2004, with an expectation that it would mark the end of that first 'horrible' year, and things would begin to get better.

So I was totally taken by surprise when I realized this wasn't the truth – at least not for me. While difficult, the first anniversary of Cale's death was not as bad as I had expected it to be. The actual day of the week, the Monday, was worse. I found myself reliving the entire day as the day progressed. On the anniversary date Cale's friends arrived again to share the day with us, but it was much lower key. We laughed and cried, hugged and shared stories. The kids went out to the pond to talk to Cale. It was hard. It was sad. But the day passed and I was left thinking "okay, that's not that bad."

Then year two started and the hurt became different. For me, it was as if the dark, heavy shroud began to lift from my head, and suddenly I could truly 'see' what had really happened and was continuing to happen. Everything became clearer, and I started to 'feel' Cale's loss in a totally different way.

My son was dead. MY SON WAS DEAD!

Anger began to swirl in me like flames, growing hotter and hotter. I hated feeling angry, but the more I tried not to be, the more angry I became. And I was angry at everyone and everything, including Cale. Although I had dealt with some anger in months past, this was different. No one and nothing was safe from my anger. I was angry that Cale had not received the right treatment early enough, and had not received enough of it. I was angry that Brad had not always been there to help me when Cale was younger, and that he had not seemed to really believe Cale suffered from mental illness at first. I was angry that I hadn't been able to find the right help; that I hadn't been able to say the right words, do the right thing, to make a difference. I was angry with the medical system, the social services system and the education system, all of whom I felt had let Cale down to some degree or another. And I was angry that Cale had chosen this way out. I was angry that I wasn't able to stop him. I was angry that I hadn't been a good mother to him. For the first time ever I wondered if God had chosen the wrong person to be Cale's mother.

It was about this time that I decided to go through Cale's school binders – the ones that I had picked up from the school the day after his death. I came across a poetry assignment and as I read my son's tortured words my anger raged into a full blown inferno. How could his obvious cry for help have been ignored? Why hadn't I asked to see his work? Why hadn't I read his words?

Chapter Six

Drowning

As my life goes on I feel as if I am drowning
in shallow water,
a long, slow, painful death.
My lungs slowly fill with water as the life leaves my body.
Blood hungry fish and vermin feast on my rotting carcass.
I am drowning.
I am waiting to be saved from my deadly fate
waiting for someone who cares to find me.
That is yet to happen and until it does
I remain here
in this sea of sorrow.

Death

Death is
amongst us.
There is no where to run
Death awaits our last dying wish
Death comes.

Bottles

Bottle by bottle
I drown my sorrow
At the bottom of every bottle
I see more and more of what my life is
and always will be
Empty.
Sitting here by myself
as I always am
the room is spinning
I can't keep my balance
and I realize this is my life
I have no balance to me
bottle by bottle.

Satan's Flame

Satan's flame
burns inside of us all
those mind altering flames
messing with our heads
We may try but cannot stop it.
It controls us;
our every word,
our every thought,
our every move.
Our lives are Satan's playground.
What are we to do?
We are under the control of Satan.

My anger was intense. Since Cale had died, I had denied being angry, but now angered bubbled up from the very core of me, like lava from a volcano. I had known that Cale had struggled with alcohol and drug issues. I had witnessed it and he had told me how he struggled. I knew he questioned the existence of God and considered himself an atheist. I knew that he heard voices that he believed were evil; that wanted him to believe he was evil. He had told me. I knew that he had struggled with self esteem issues and low self confidence; that he had felt he didn't fit in and didn't belong; that he would never amount to anything. I knew all these things. Cale had told me. I knew that he wanted to be more like his brother; that he wanted to have a relationship with a girl like Adam had with Ange. I knew that Cale felt like he was always failing his father and I. I knew these things because Cale had told me.

I also knew that for years I had tried to get help through the school system, only to be told Cale's problems were just behavioural. With the exception of a few teachers and educators who saw something in Cale that others did not, most felt he was a disruption, a discipline problem. The few who 'saw' something were locked in a system that didn't budge and seemed to believe that children couldn't have mental illness, therefore everything was behavioural, and therefore changeable.

Now, sitting before me in his own words, was proof of just how much Cale had been suffering, and his English teacher had not even noticed. He received a good mark on the poetry project, but no red flags had come up when the assignment was read and marked. How could that be?

The anger in me was unbelievable, and there were days when it threatened to consume me. How could any teacher read these words and not pick up the phone and contact us, his parents? How could any teacher see the academic value of my son's words, but not see the pain and suffering behind them?

Shortly before Cale died he had made a career decision to become some type of counselor and work with teenagers and young adults. He felt he had something to offer them; he could understand what they were going through. A friend **Drew, had helped him see how much he had to give. Drew had become a great confidant to Cale. One night Cale and I talked about this decision and how he might carry it out. The next day Cale came home from school saying he had changed his mind. He looked beaten.

"I can't be a counselor, mom," he had said. "I don't know what I was thinking."

When I questioned Cale further I learned he had told one of his teachers about his decision. The teacher had laughed at Cale, in front of his classmates, and made a joke about the unlikelihood of him becoming a counselor. Cale was totally defeated. I was devastated…and angry.

That anger came back in full force now, and I spent my days trying to quell it. I had by this time returned to work at Windsor Essex Family Network as Family to Family Coordinator and was helping to expand a family to family support program for families with individuals with disabilities. A large number of the calls to our office involved children with mental health challenges and education issues. My anger grew as I listened to parents tell of their child being ignored, ridiculed or sidelined by teachers, educational assistants, principals and others. My son had experienced this over and over throughout his elementary school education. One of Cale's elementary school teachers, in fact, had told me that Cale, perhaps, was not worth helping as some kids simply can't be helped. I was frustrated and overwhelmed by the fact that although close to two years had passed since Cale's death, little seemed to have changed.

Most of all, I was just angry that I no longer had my son. I was tired of people telling me how good I looked and how well I was doing. I didn't care what they thought. I didn't care that others felt that more than a year had passed and I should get on with my life. I just wanted Cale back. I missed my conversations with him; I missed his smile and his wacky sense of humour. I missed the weird food concoctions he would prepare for supper. I even missed his anger, his irritability and volatility. I missed the way he would come up behind me and cross his arms on my head, leaning his chin on his arm; and how this usually ended with him dropping his arm down to hug me from behind. I missed never knowing what colour his hair would be when I got home from work, or if he would have any hair left. I missed his childlike exuberance when he was excited about something. I missed his crazy clothes and his crazy ideas. I missed our debates, discussions and arguments. I missed his voice, his sound, his presence, his passion, his volatility, his anger, his outrage at injustice, his rebellion. Life was way too quiet without Cale. I wanted him back. I didn't want to hear that wasn't possible. I didn't want to be told it would get better. I just wanted him back.

I went to my doctor often during this time. I had struggled with depression on and off through most of my life, so I was aware of the need to monitor my medication, especially with the additional stress I was under. My doctor assured me that I was doing well, considering my situation. He urged me to be gentle with myself; to give myself time.

Cale's friends continued to help and in September 2004 I attended the graduation of Kelly Hutchins and Mike Hicks. I watched from the back of the room and although I was proud of Kelly and Mike, my heart ached for my son.

As the names of the graduates were called out, and the 'S' names were started then completed – without Cale's name being called - I was overcome by sadness. I could visibly see my son standing in the spot he should have occupied. I was torn between joy for the students who were moving on and forward in their lives and anger and sadness that my son was not present, and would never graduate.

And my anger continued to grow in the coming months, being displaced for brief periods of time by intense depression. But the depression rarely lasted long before the anger kicked in. I knew how to handle the depression. I had dealt with it many times before. The anger was different. I didn't know how to handle the anger. I had always avoided anger, worried that if I showed my anger I would scare people away, or bad things would happen.

Now it took over my life. I couldn't sleep. I couldn't write, and writing had been my escape and my passion since I was a little girl. I couldn't think. I went to work and couldn't wait until the day was done. I was exhausted and wanted to sleep, but when I went to bed, sleep eluded me. I wasn't interested in socializing with friends. I wasn't interested in conversation, or reading or listening to music. I wasn't interested in sitting out by the pond, enjoying the peaceful surroundings. I wasn't interested in sex or intimacy. I wasn't interested in anything I had previously enjoyed. My anger was all consuming.

And I couldn't get the image of the last night with Cale out of my mind. For almost two years I had tried to put the image aside, knowing that the bathroom was an essential room in our home. I kept telling myself I just needed to deal with it. Now, however, the entire evening would play in my mind like a movie in slow motion the moment I stepped into the bathroom. Every trip to the bathroom was filled with mind and body memories of everything that had taken place. I never wanted to see the bathroom again, and worried that I could not continue to live in our home.

Yet I couldn't bring myself to talk to Brad about the situation. Brad had worked so hard to build up his business and had, in fact, constructed a $20,000 addition mere months before Cale died. I feared his anger if I asked to move. Worse, I feared that he would move just for me, and later despise me, or he would refuse to move, and I would be forced to leave on my own. At the same time I knew we could not afford to renovate our bathroom and change its appearance enough to stop the memories from destroying me. I believed my only option was to deal with it, and I knew I wasn't doing that well.

About a week before Cale's 18th birthday on November 27, 2004 I went on an overnight trip to the Pinery in Grand Bend, Ontario with my sister and Peggy. Each of us was dealing with different situations at the time and all needed a break. Once at the park Peggy decided to walk on her own while Joanne and I headed off through the trails. Extremely worried about me, and knowing she had nothing to lose Joanne set about convincing me that I had no choice but to talk to Brad about the situation. In her judgment, not only was I harming myself by not speaking up, I was being unfair to Brad. Given the chance, she said, Brad would want to do whatever was necessary to help me. She believed Brad would see moving and having to establish his business at a new location as a better option than watching me continue to live in such pain. Usually gentle and compassionate in our conversations, Joanne was firm and slightly abrasive, telling me I needed to deal with this. As she talked we lost our way and ended up wandering the park for several hours longer than we had expected. It just meant several more hours that she continued to talk to me. Later she would tell me that she knew she was pushing me; knew she was hurting me, but knew also that it was necessary.

"It was as if Cale was telling me what to say," she would tell me later.

I was not convinced that I had the right to ask such a huge change of Brad. This was his home and his livelihood. How could I ask him to leave?

The debate and turmoil continued to bubble and brew inside me. I thought I was loosing my mind. It all came to a head a few nights later. I was laying in bed, again unable to sleep, when I heard Cale's voice saying "Mom, wake up. I need to talk to you."

Astounded by the clarity of Cale's voice, I sat up and looked towards the foot of the bed where Cale had stood a hundred times when he couldn't sleep. There he stood again, this time surrounded by a faint bluish-yellow light. Although I was aware that I should be frightened, I was not. Instead, I felt strangely at peace as Cale told me it was time for me to let the night of his death go so that we both could be at peace. As he spoke those words I understood that in leaving the bathroom as it was the night Cale died, I was holding onto my last encounter with Cale, horrible as it was.

"Do what you need to do" Cale whispered. "Do what you need to do."

He then smiled at me and slowly disappeared until the room was once again black, as if he had never been there.

Any resolve I had was gone. I got out of bed and went downstairs. Sitting in the living room I started sobbing uncontrollably. Brad woke up a few minutes later and followed me downstairs, and it was then that I finally told Brad what was happening to me. Once I explained the horror I felt each time I entered the bathroom, Brad told me he had no way of understanding what I had gone through, but wanted only what was best for me. Once I let go of the anxiety I had been holding, I realized I didn't want to move. I did, however, want to renovate the bathroom. Brad was, as Joanne had predicted, interested only in doing whatever was necessary to ease my anxiety.

In the days to come we made a decision together to gut the bathroom and renovate. Our goal would be to turn it into a peaceful sanctuary, with a large whirlpool tub, shelves for candles, beautiful lighting and décor. We would deal with the finances somehow.

The day of Cale's 18th birthday brought another wave of anger, and another Cale-inspired message from Joanne – a message that would ultimately bring me intense healing.

We were supposed to attend a family gathering on Cale's birthday, and Brad and I had at first considered not attending. Later we decided to bring 18 helium balloons to the get together, and invite people to join us in letting the balloons go in the evening.

Joanne told me, in no uncertain terms, that she felt it was a bad idea. She was worried that Brad and I would be hurt, and people would feel obligated to participate.

"Cale's death is over for everyone else, Diane," she said, adding that not everyone celebrates the birthdays of loved ones who are alive, let alone those who have died.

I was, she said, setting myself up to get hurt.

Anger raged through me as I hung up the phone. I grabbed a large porcelain planter that we had received at Cale's funeral, and lifting it above my head, slammed it down onto the floor of the living room. The planter shattered, pieces flew everywhere and my dog, who had been sleeping near me, jumped up and ran up the stairs, unsure of my anger. The rage vibrated through my body. I was horrified by what I had done; even more horrified by the intense, burning rage, but could do nothing to stop it.

Brad and I did attend the family gathering and it was clear to me that Joanne had been right. We would not have been able to hold a celebration for Cale that evening; it wasn't our party, it wasn't the right timing and some people would not have been receptive.

It took some more time, and more processing, for me to realize just how right Joanne had been and to understand the full impact of her words. Later, when I went to thank her for having the courage to face my wrath and speak her truth, she would tell me that again, it seemed as though Cale were talking through her. For me, it was a sad, but necessary realization that life goes on for others in a different way than for those who lose a loved one. From that moment forward I was careful to pick and choose who I allowed to see my sadness, grief and vulnerability

On the evening of Cale's birthday, after attending the family gathering, Brad and I celebrated quietly at home, letting 18 white helium balloons fly into the black night near the pond. While 17 balloons headed northeast, one of the balloons headed the opposite way, getting caught in some weeds between two barns. Brad and I both felt it was Cale, choosing to be different like he used to, and letting us know he was present. Brad untangled the balloon and it, too, floated off into the black night.

The next morning Brad handed me a hammer and I entered the bathroom. Without a second thought I began smashing the ceramic tile floor, releasing, with every swing, the anger, sadness, grief and despair that had been building for so long. Pieces of tile flew in all directions and a cloud of dust quickly filled the room. The renovation of my bathroom, and the rebuilding of my psyche, had begun.

Over the course of the renovation Cale continued to give us 'messages' to let us know he was with us. When cleaning out the bathroom vanity, I found a small chain link ring Cale used to wear, in the back of one of the draws. I slipped it on my finger and wore it for weeks, before storing it in my jewelry chest. While pulling out one of the walls, we found a pile of dinky cars at the bottom between the studs. Years before Adam and Cale had dropped them through a hole upstairs while they were playing. Then, when Brad and I went to pick out our ceramic tile for the floor, we chose four designs that we liked. We brought all four home to match against our sink and tub. Both of us chose the same one, without hesitation. The name of the tile was Kale.

As we renovated the bathroom my spirit took flight. Nothing could have been more therapeutic. I felt free, light and alive for the first time in a very, very long time.

Cale and I enjoyed one of his presents at Christmas in 1987.

Adam, left, at age 2 posed with his brother Cale, 4 months.

Cale enjoyed a bubblebath while our family was staying at a hotel.

Enjoying a petting zoo during a trip to African Lion Safari.

This picture was taken at school in Junior or Senior Kindergarten.

This is one of our earlier family photos.

'A Future Star' – Cale looked very determined
when he posed for this photo.

Cale blows out candles on his cake at his 4th birthday party.

Cale, right, and his father silhouetted against the setting sun while
fishing on Eagle Lake in South River, Ontario.

Cale, left, posed with his cousins (clockwise) Charlie, Marnie, brother Adam, and Kari at his Gramma Dolan's 60th birthday party. Their shirts read Happy 60th Birthday Gramma.

Cale's interest in varied hairstyles startedin Grade School.

Cale paused under a bluff at the Elora Gorge in Elora, Ontario, while hiking with his father and brother.

Cale worked on a project comparing the
viscosity of various motor oils.

Cale and Adam befriended the tree frogs while visiting their Aunt
Ghislaine and Uncle Jim's campground in Crossville, Tennessee.

An avid Red Wings fan, Cale posed with the Stanley Cup and Craig
and Roberta McCarty, Darren McCarty's parents.

Cale wore his Red Wings jersey to a Red Wing Alumni Charity
Game in order to solicit autographs.

Brad, Adam and Cale enjoyed conversation
while in Tennessee for Christmas 2000.

While on a trip to Tennessee's Smokey Mountains Cale paused to climb this wall.

And sat at the top enjoying the senic view.

Cale enjoyed a stroll in the river while we were visiting the
Smokey Mountains in Tennessee.

Cale, in his last school picture before he died.

Cale, with his brother Adam and his girlfriend Angela at his Uncle Norm's wedding in November 2002, four months before his death.

This picture, taken at a friends house, was the last picture taken of Cale before he died.

Never 2B Forgotten

Never 2B Forgotten

Cale Simon
November 27, 1986 – April 7, 2003

Cale was not just another person in this world; he was a true individual. Known to some as "Ziggy," Cale was different from most students. Many people saw him as a freak or as an outcast because one could always point him out in a crowd either by his spiky hair (or lack of), by his piercings, or else by the anarchy symbols he wore. But Cale wasn't an outcast to us; he was part of a small family of students who will miss him dearly. It's hard to go outside without imagining "Ziggy" there. He will be sadly missed by all who took the time to know him.

Written by Mike Hicks

I watch the sun go down like everyone of us
I'm hoping that the dawn will bring a sign
A better place for those who will come after us
This time

from "Dreamer" by Ozzy Osborne

Photos at left provided by Mrs. Diane Simon

In Memoriam

Now that you're gone, you flew with wings
If you listen carefully, you can hear him sing.
I hope that you have no regrets for what you did in the past,
Even though you're gone our friendship will always last.

You and I had good times.
At night, I see your star that shines.
I really wish that you didn't say goodbye.
My love for you as a friend will never die.

I know I'll see you again someday.
When I do, I hope that you're okay.
I wish instead that you were alive for many years.
When I think of you, I cry a lot of tears.

You'll always be a good friend of mine.
I know that I'll see you again sometime.
I know it's time to let you go.
I just can't and I won't.

"Goodbye" by Jamie-Lee Taggart, written for Cale

RIGHT: LDSS students lined Talbot Street to pay their respects to Cale. FAR RIGHT: Mike Hicks honoured Cale by playing "Amazing Grace" during the funeral procession.

Photos by Yila Nichols

Forever 2B Loved

Forever 2B Loved

This wonderful memorial was designed by his friends and students and published in the 2003 high school yearbook.

Chapter Seven

It was around this time, heading towards the second anniversary of Cale's death, that I sat down with Cale's baby record book and a box of photographs and allowed myself to really remember my son.

Cale was born at 8:18 a.m. on Thursday, November 27, 1986. He weighed 8 pounds 15 ½ ounces and was 21 inches long. His brother, born in March of the previous year was 7 pounds 3 ounces, 21 inches long. I remember wondering how they could be the same length, yet such different weights. It became clear when we compared Cale's hospital picture with Adam's. Cale's head, topped with white blond hair, looked like it was twice the size of Adam's. With his screwed up facial expression and his balled fists, Cale looked like a miniature wrestler.

My pregnancy with Cale had been very difficult and anxiety-ridden. With morning sickness plaguing me for the entire nine months, I gained only 18 pounds. Cale was very, very active in utero, much more than I had remembered Adam being. I also endured massive migraines for which I was hospitalized, and in my sixth month contracted a uterine infection which caused hours of premature labour. I was treated both in the hospital and as an outpatient with antibiotics, gravol and painkillers for the headaches.

I remember one day, while in the hospital, questioning the neurosurgeon about the medications, especially the painkillers. He assured me they were safe and would not hurt the baby.

Although Adam had been born by emergency C-Section, I had decided to attempt a natural delivery with Cale. About ten hours after labour began I had been given an epidural and everything seemed to be progressing fine when Cale went into distress and his heartbeat disappeared from the monitor. An emergency C-Section was ordered and the specialist was called.

In the 45 minutes that followed, while I was prepped for surgery and we awaited the obstetrician, I watched the monitor closely, looking for signs of Cale's heartbeat. I held conversations with God, and made a pact. I asked for my child to be born healthy and strong, and vowed that I would have no more children. I would be satisfied with this new baby and my 20-month old son Adam. I promised to be a better person. I promised to do something good with my life and to be kind to people. I made all those promises that people make in times of tragedy. It was the longest 45 minutes of my life.

God answered my prayers and Cale was born healthy. Hearing him cry for the first time was a blessing, and all seemed fine. He slept well and ate well for the first few days, and he and I remained in the hospital for a week.

Adam had been a calm, 'at peace,' happy baby, sleeping through the night at two weeks of age and playing for hours on the floor or in a playpen near me. He loved lying in his playpen outside and watching the leaves and birds.

It soon became apparent to Brad and I that Cale would not be the same. He was not a good sleeper, and while he ate well generally, he often suffered from tummy aches and colic. Nights would pass when Cale did not sleep at all, or slept for only 15 or 20 minutes at a time. Often the only way to get him to sleep at all was to lay him on my chest and stomach. Then, the heat from my body seemed to calm his stomach and allow him to sleep. Often Brad would return home after midnight from the afternoon shift to find Cale and I asleep on the recliner, Cale laying across my stomach and chest. At other times the only way I could soothe him was to hold him tight against my body while standing, and swing him back and forth as fast as possible. It was almost as if I needed to numb his mind with the constant movement before he could fall asleep. He did not sleep through the night until 22 months of age, and then only rarely.

Cale was almost two years old and Adam 3 ½ when I returned to the work force, as a fulltime reporter/photographer for the Leamington Post. Although I loved the job, it would be a difficult five years between illnesses I was struggling with and the situation with Cale. As young as he was I was already witnessing issues of great concern to me as a mother.

Cale would often become very angry at his brother and young cousins. On one occasion he scratched his brother's back with his fingernails, leaving three or four deep long welts across Adam's back. Initially he was not remorseful. It wasn't until some time later, and a lot of talking with him, that he realized what he had done. When that seemed to 'click' he became extremely upset and remorseful, certain that Adam would not like him anymore.

Despite his young age, Cale's anxiety level was incredibly high. He constantly worried about what might go wrong and was certain that what could go wrong would. He struggled with understanding normal social interaction at school and with friends, and often would become angry with teasing and the necessity for taking turns. He was fidgety and nervous and had a great deal of trouble sitting still for any length of time. He struggled greatly in the structured school setting, finding it difficult to concentrate and focus; finding the distraction around him unbearable.

And he was filled with an unbelievable rage. From an early age he suffered episodes of rage which would come on with the fury of a hurricane, and nothing I could do or say would stop them. It was as if, once started, they had to run their course. He kicked walls and threw things, pushed and struck playmates. Terrified that he would hurt himself or someone else I would often hold him tight as he screamed, roared, swore, kicked and struggled. Brad and I often disagreed with what was causing the rages and how to handle them. I often felt that Brad was too stern. He often felt I was too soft, and let Cale get away with too much. We struggled to find a common meeting ground.

As a child, Cale's rages would dissipate as quickly as they began, and Cale would collapse like a rag doll in my arms. He would breakdown, crying uncontrollably. The first time he spoke, in veiled terms of suicide was after one of these episodes. He was seven years old, and curled up in my lap, sobbing.

"What's wrong with me?" he asked. "Why am I so bad? I don't want to be here. I just want to die."

I remember my heart shattering. My seven-year-old son felt that life was not worth living. What could possibly be happening in his tiny mind to make him believe this. I was terrified of losing him and determined to get help.

I tried hard to convince Cale he wasn't bad; and promised I would do whatever needed to be done to get help. Cale remained quiet in my arms, drained of energy, limp.

As strong as Cale's anger and rage were, his compassion, humour and intelligence were twice as strong. A very deep sensitivity ran through his little body, and he simply could not understand why children were starving and hurt, or animals were suffering. On a trip out of town to one of Adam's hockey tournaments, we were leaving the hotel. As we passed the garbage pail, I threw out a partial box of donuts and an almost full box of cereal. Heading towards our car Cale turned around in time to see a homeless man taking the left over food. He was devastated, and wanted us to go back and give him money or buy him some more food. He just didn't understand how the world could be so unjust; how some could be without food or homes or basic necessities. On another trip to Detroit to see a stage show, he was moved by the homeless people begging for money on the streets, and angry because I could not give them all money. It was difficult to explain, in terms that his young mind could understand, why we couldn't help everyone and needed to be careful as well.

Our house would have been a haven for every stray, injured or sick animal if Cale and Adam had their way, and it often was. While Adam loved animals, like his father he seemed to have a common sense understanding of what was feasible and what was not. Cale, on the other hand, was very much like me and driven one hundred percent by his heart. As a family we rescued kittens and dogs and nursed birds, bunnies and raccoons back to health. We also rescued a grey heron with a broken leg (my idea) and a seagull with a broken leg (Cale's idea). For days after dropping the seagull off at a Leamington veterinarian, Cale insisted on daily trips to make sure he was doing okay. The bird was later released back into the wild. Over the years our humble abode was home to lizards, guinea pigs and two small snakes, belonging to Adam, which would eventually grow to be about ten feet in length. I joked often with Adam and Cale that they were lucky to have a mom who loved snakes.

My most vivid memory of Cale and animals involved traveling along the Essex Bypass towards Leamington in the middle of a massive thunderstorm one afternoon. With little visibility I found myself swerving at the last moment to avoid striking a huge snapping turtle in the middle of the road.

Cale became distraught, certain that if we did not move the turtle off the road it would be hit and killed. We returned to the spot where we had seen the turtle and, as lighting flashed across the sky, thunder crashed and rain pelted us, Cale and I proceeded to 'convince' the reptile to get off the highway. Using an umbrella and a long piece of cardboard I found in the car, we gently nudged the large fellow, as Cale spoke quietly trying to convince him we were not trying to hurt him. As his large, steel-trap jaws crashed down on the umbrella and cardboard again and again, we made certain to keep our toes and fingers far out of the way.

By the time we were done, 'our' turtle was in the ditch, happy I assume. Our cardboard box was half eaten and the plastic tip of my umbrella had been shattered by the incredible reptilian jaws. Cale and I were soaking wet and covered in mud…and Cale was smiling.

Chapter Eight

I began searching for medical help for Cale, and parenting help for me, when my boys were quite young. I had grown up as a crown ward of a Southwestern Ontario children's aid society, and suffered through more than 20 placements before a final long term foster placement. Through experience I knew all too well what I did not want to do as a parent. I would not beat, abuse, sexually abuse or verbally degrade my children. I would not abandon them. And I would never, ever allow them to be taken away from me. I knew how to love them but I didn't know much about parenting them.

In the early years of Cale's life, and the early school years, I called agencies and organizations and services providers. I called doctors and therapists. I read books and talked to friends, clergy and anyone else I thought might have insight I didn't have. Everywhere I turned I heard the same things – we don't deal with these kinds of problems; he doesn't fit our criteria; he's too old for our service. It's all behavioural. You're not parenting right. The educational system looked upon Cale as a behavioural problem; I could not find the help we needed to prove otherwise.

At age seven Cale was seen by another specialist. I don't remember whether he was a psychiatrist or a pediatrician specializing in children's mental health. While it had been suggested that Cale had ADHD, this doctor felt that might not be the only diagnosis. He believed that Cale could be suffering from bipolar disorder as well. The doctor, however, did not wish to treat Cale's ADHD with medication and due to his age, and the lack of testing on children, felt medication could not be used for bipolar disorder either. His recommendation was to help Cale learn to deal with the ADHD symptoms and limitations. Unspoken, in my mind, was to just forget he might have bipolar disorder.

We continued to seek help for Cale, and I found myself sitting on the doorstep of a psychiatrist in London. After meeting with us once, he agreed that Cale was suffering from ADHD and possibly bipolar disorder but was not willing to take Cale on as a patient. We then turned to **Dr. Richards, head of the children's department at a London psychiatric facility. Dr. Richards felt Cale was suffering from depression and suggested a tri-cyclic antidepressant which we tried for several months. Cale's depression seemed to improve on the antidepressant, but he became much more irritable, agitated and his ability to concentrate decreased significantly. Dr. Richards stopped the antidepressant and began treating Cale with Ritalin. Cale continued to see Dr. Richards for several months, but traveling to London, and not being able to access Dr. Richards during times of crisis created great difficulty. Moreover, I questioned the diagnosis of ADHD, and felt very strongly that something more significant was taking place.

In the fall of 1996 during a long episode of rage, depression and anxiety, Cale left me a note alluding to his desire to kill himself. He planned, he said, to jump out the window of his second story bedroom. Terrified, I took him to the emergency room at a Windsor hospital, begging for help. The attending doctor 'assured' me I didn't have to worry; that children Cale's age were just looking for attention when they left notes like this. I was still terrified, and remember thinking my son should not have to threaten suicide to get attention. I remember asking the doctor when I should start believing Cale wasn't just looking for attention... perhaps when he actually jumped?

As a result of that visit we received a referral for Cale to a children's mental health facility. Following a meeting with a social worker, Cale was scheduled to see a child psychiatrist, **Dr. Don Campbell. This meeting took place in November 1996. Due to DR. Campbell's intense schedule

I was unable to meet with him, but he forwarded his report to **Dr. Mary Timmins, our family physician. In his report Dr. Campbell stated he believed Cale to be a highly anxious child who was suffering from severe depression. He suggested Cale be treated with the antidepressant Prozac, which was then prescribed by Dr. Timmins. Although Brad and I hated the though of Cale being on more medication, we agreed that we needed to try; that things couldn't get worse for Cale. Even then I feared that doing nothing would lead to the death of my son.

When Cale first began taking the Prozac suggested by Dr. Campbell it did appear to have somewhat of a calming effect on him, but only for a very short time. Cale then began suffering from severe stomach aches, headaches and uncontrollable shaking. Cale's dosage of Prozac was decreased and the physical symptoms disappeared. However his depression, anxiety, frustration and rage continued.

In addition, around this same time Cale was also seen by a psychologist who believed Cale's entire situation was caused by Brad's and my parenting skills – or lack there of. In particular he intimated that it was doubtful I could possess any proper parenting skills having grown up as I had, in the care of a children's aid society; that I was, in fact, the main reason Cale was struggling so greatly.

"What do you expect with your history?" he asked me, bluntly.

I left his office wondering if I was, in fact, to blame.

Days later I returned to the facility not to see the psychologist, but to consult with his supervisor. I made it clear I would not tolerate another meeting with the doctor, and that he was not to be allowed near my son. I stated, clearly, that if I could make it this far in life having survived the abuse of my childhood, I sure as hell could learn what I needed to learn to help my child and be a good parent. As far as I was concerned, I was already half-way there. I loved my children unconditionally and thanks to my past knew quite clearly what I did not want to do.

This time period was, perhaps, one of the main turning points in our struggle to access proper medical and psychiatric treatment for Cale. Whatever had been simmering below the surface of the volcano seemed to erupt in late 1996, early 1997. It was at this time that I decided to document Cale's moods, to see if there was some type of cycle.

As in his early childhood, Cale continued to have a difficult time falling and staying asleep. He often spoke of feeling like he was being watched by somebody, or something. I often had to stay in the room with him until he fell asleep. He was experiencing major episodes of rage, followed by the sadness I described earlier. This would often dissipate and Cale would be relatively fine for about a week. He would then become more and more irritable until he had another episode of rage…and the cycle would begin again. Overall, however, Cale appeared melancholic. He seemed, always, to be tense and had difficulty making decisions.

Cale was also very attached to me and seemed to suffer from great anxiety concerning me. If I was fifteen minutes late he would become anxious and begin calling me.

School was a nightmare for Cale from the very earliest days on. In junior kindergarten he started becoming physically ill each morning when it was time to get on the bus for school. After days of talking and working with his teachers, we finally determined another student had ripped Cale's Halloween costume, and Cale thought the boy was mad at him.

As early as Grade 1 he began getting in trouble for not sitting still, not getting his work done, not paying attention. He couldn't handle teasing; simply didn't comprehend how it worked, and he reacted with hurt and anger, lashing out at other children in violence. He soon became the target of bullies, and would often retaliate in anger, mostly with words but often by pushing or hitting. It was rare that the child who instigated an incident would be held accountable. Instead, because of his retaliation, Cale would be penalized, and often was not even allowed to explain what had taken place. At home his anger often turned inward to self hate and shame. By then, I usually couldn't even work through the situation with him to determine what could have been handled differently. By then, self loathing had taken over. Over the entire course of his elementary school Cale felt he had no one to turn to, with the exception of a very few teachers, and one principal and vice principal.

Even when Cale was clearly trying to change and make better choices it often seemed to end in disaster for him. I was called to the school on one occasion when he had kicked a garbage can in anger. In my mind it was a huge step up from the month before when he had tried to kick another child. Yes, it was still wrong, but it was a garbage can. It was not seen that way by the school.

Cale's days at school were filled with bullying, teasing, assignments he didn't understand, fighting to stay on track and focus, angry outbursts, anxiety and agitation. His evenings were spent grappling with homework he couldn't understand, more angry outburst, depression, anxiety, agitation, self loathing and tears, lots of tears. And always there were the rages, when books flew and words flew and Cale's anger oozed out in every direction. School authorities seemed to feel these were totally behavioural in nature, as were his other issues. I fought to get the help we needed to prove there was something else taking place.

For my part I spent my days trying to get my work done, trying to find help for Cale on my breaks and lunch hours, but waiting, constantly, on pins and needles for my pager to beep. Then I would be summoned to school to pick Cale up and take him home.

Daily, often hourly, I wondered what I needed to do to help this incredibly intelligent child reach his potential. What could I do to get people to see what was beneath the fear, anxiety, depression and anger? It didn't seem to matter what I tried, or said, or did. The phone calls to come get him just kept on coming. Cale hit someone today. Cale yelled at someone today. Cale wouldn't sit still today. Cale didn't complete his assignment today. Cale wasn't allowed to go out for recess because he didn't bring his homework in, and got mad and yelled at the teacher today. Cale wouldn't sing the national anthem this morning. Cale forgot his glasses today. Cale wouldn't eat his lunch today.

Day after day I would go to the school to get Adam and Cale and Cale would hold his emotions in check until we reached the car. Then he would begin to cry, at first angry with the events of the day. This, however, would soon turned to self loathing and shame, and he would beginning questioning what was wrong with him.

The trauma of these early years all came to a head early one April when I was called to Cale's school, where Cale had been involved in a 'serious' situation. I believe Cale was in Grade 4 or 5. I cannot remember what the issue was; what Cale had done. It may have been just more of the same. I just know it was the straw that broke the camel's back for me, if not for Cale.

When I arrived at school, it was obvious that Cale's teacher, principal and some of his classmates were furious with Cale. Other classmates were keeping their distance from Cale, who stood on one side of the room alone, looking like a caged animal. He was agitated, jittery and terrified, his eyes flashing with fear. When he saw me he ran into my arms, crying and holding tight. Unlike normal, he said nothing; just cried. I didn't even stop to talk to the teacher. Holding Cale in one arm, I gathered his things and on the spot made the painful decision to remove him from school. He wasn't gaining anything from being at school; he felt overwhelmed, uncomfortable and ostracized. He wasn't getting help to deal with his depression, rage, frustration or self esteem issues. And I was exhausted. I just couldn't fight the school system any longer. I knew I needed to regain my strength to get Cale the help he needed.

It was just one of many difficult decisions we were forced to make in the coming weeks. During a visit to his endocrinologist, who was treating Cale for familial high cholesterol, blood tests confirmed Cale suffered from low thyroid function. I had requested the test based on symptoms I had observed, and the fact that thyroid problems ran on Brad's side of the family.

Once Cale was diagnosed with low thyroid function, I began researching the condition, which I had been told could contribute to depression. While I wasn't able to locate a great deal of information, what I did learn was frightening. Hypothyroidism, or low thyroid function, could be a contributing factor in everything from mood swings and depression to rage, decreased growth, anxiety, and more.

Suddenly we were faced with an entire new barrage of questions? Did Cale indeed have ADHD and/or Bipolar? If so, was his thyroid condition making them worse? If not, were the symptoms actually caused by his thyroid? Was his high anxiety a result of hypothyroidism? How in the world were we ever going to figure out what was really happening with our son?

I was exhausted and terrified. There were many times I remember sitting and crying, thinking I just couldn't do this anymore. Somehow, from somewhere I would get another burst of determination and carry on.

And I was angry. We seemed to be getting different answers everywhere we turned. Brad and I were very concerned with the fact that Cale could be receiving treatment with extremely powerful drugs for depression and ADHD, when it might, in fact, be his thyroid causing or contributing to the problem.

Dr. Campbell, however, seemed unconcerned with this. In fact, Dr. Campbell performed no follow up on Cale for more than four months after he placed the order to start Cale on Prozac. After learning of Cale's diagnosis of hypothyroidism, I left two frantic messages with the social worker who acted as our liaison to Dr. Campbell. I begged for an appointment for Cale to talk about this new development, and my concerns.

I received a phone call from the social worker informing me to continue with my plans to have Cale treated for hypothyroidism through his endocrinologist, and to 'keep them informed."

Dr. Campbell's response was frustrating, and disappointing. I had total confidence in Cale's endocrinologist's ability to deal with the thyroid issue. What I questioned was how it might affect Cale's psychological issues, and whether those medications might need adjusting. I also believed that even if Cale required the Ritalin and Prozac, he needed to be followed by a psychiatrist. I worried that he was on these medications and a full assessment had never been completed. He had never had an EEG or psychological assessment. And, I wanted help for my whole family – counselling, training, assistance to learn how to help Cale cope with his situation and access the skills and self confidence he needed to complete school and be successful.

At this same time the trials of raising a child with severe mental health challenges was taking its toll on our home life. Brad and I seemed to be arguing more than working together, and I felt often like a single parent, mostly due to Brad's straight afternoon shifts. I attended most medical, counselling and education appointments for the boys on my own.

In April 1997, when Cale was 10, I decided to contact a well-renowned and esteemed London psychiatrist **Dr. Susan Marks. I'm not sure how I had learned about Dr. Marks, but other parents assured me she was the best, and would know what to do. I figured the two hour drive to London was worth it if I could get help for Cale and our family.

Desperate for help, I prepared a letter outlining the past years.

"I am desperately trying to find help for my 10-year-old son, Cale. I met with our family physician today, and she is in support of me contacting you, as my husband and I feel Cale's situation has reached a critical point. Last Friday Brad (my husband) and I had to take our son out of school because of situations which may be behavioural in nature, but which we strongly feel may have either a medical or psychiatric basis or are being contributed to by a medical or psychiatric problem. I am terrified I am going to lose my child…it is not uncommon for him to speak of not wanting to live, of being worthless, of hating himself because he can't control his anger. This child, although 10, crawls into my arms and begs me to help him; begs me to tell him what is wrong with him. It tears my heart apart, because I can't give him the answers we both need.

This has been going on for many years, but I will just quickly fill you in on what has happened in the last six months. Cale is a sweet, wonderful, intelligent child. He is kind and loving and adores animals. He has always had difficulty with the academics of schooling, yet is so intelligent in his conversations that we have difficulty understanding the gap between the two. He has been tested on a one-to-one basis with a resource teacher at school and has scored at or above his age level in every category, but cannot seem to carry this through to practical work in a classroom setting. He cannot concentrate on schoolwork or any type of project for any length of time. He is often depressed and, as I said, has spoke of suicide, although always in veiled terms. He gets frustrated very, very easily and is easily distracted and frustrated by noises around him. He often believes people don't like him or are taunting him, and is extremely defensive. For example, if he sees a group of his classmates are laughing, he immediately thinks they are laughing at him. He worries about everything. I seem to be the only person in his life that he believes does not dislike him, and I believe I am the only person in his life he trusts and believes loves him.

Perhaps the most traumatizing aspect of my son's situation is the fact that when his frustration reaches a certain level (this often occurs quickly and as a result of small situations) he will explode into these uncontrollable rages. Nothing helps. We cannot talk to him, we cannot calm him down. It is almost like he has to allow them to run their course. When in these rages, he is like a different child. He screams, shouts, throws things, curses. There have been days that I have simply grabbed him, hugged him and held on, not knowing what else to do. When I do so, I find that he is shaking with rage. When it is over, he is simply spent, as if he has no strength left. Often, afterwards, he will not remember specific details – things he shouted or threw – but he does remember the rage and anger.

This is the same child who will make me stop my car to help a turtle across the road so it won't get hit be a car. This is the same child who will cry when he sees a child abused on television. Cale is the first one in my family to sense when I have had a bad day or am tired or a little down.

If Cale were not remorseful following an episode like this, I would have a much harder time justifying it as anything beyond a behavioural problem. But I have sat and held this child while he sobbed in despair, begging me to please help him. Often following an episode he will say he doesn't want to live, or doesn't deserve to live; that we would be better off without him.

My son is 10 years old and he is living in some kind of hell that I cannot understand and cannot help him through.

He was diagnosed as having Attention Deficit Hyperactivity Disorder several years ago and was placed on Ritalin, which he still receives. Last fall, after he left me a written note alluding to killing himself, I took him to emergency at a Windsor hospital and begged for help. (I was told on that visit that children often are looking for attention when they leave such notes)

I mailed the letter off to Dr. Marks. At the same time I sent a similar message to **Dr. Deborah Smythe, a local pediatrician specializing in behavioural issues, who I had heard about. Dr. Smythe agreed to see

Cale, and continued to see him until the time of his death. Throughout the coming years Dr. Smythe spent countless hours working diligently with us to try to provide the best treatment available to Cale. Perhaps most importantly, she listened to Cale, Brad and I, and was always quick to acknowledge Cale's strengths, intelligence and sense of humour.

An appointment was scheduled for Dr. Marks, in August of 1997, but before then Cale's situation reached a crisis point. In June 1997, Cale crashed emotionally and psychologically following a series of stressors including moving to a new house, a car accident in which my car was totaled and I was injured, our dog, Shadow, being hit be a car and seriously hurt. His anxiety level dramatically increased, and he went from being deliriously happy one minute to sad and forlorn the next. After more than a week passed with less than an hour of sleep per night, I took Cale to emergency. A kind, compassionate emergency room doctor noted that more than anything, Cale needed some sleep. He sent us home with Chloral Hydrate, and I was thankful that Cale would finally get some rest.

The medication, however, appeared to have the opposite effect on Cale, and he became hyper and highly agitated. He was angry, crying, yelling. He screamed about not wanting to live, saying everyone would be better off without him.

At one point he headed off to his room, and a short time later I went to check on him. As I entered the room, he was climbing out the window, with only one leg and part of his lower torso in the room. The rest of his body hung two floors about he ground. I somehow managed to grab Cale and pull him back into the room and onto his water bed, where I held him for what seemed like hours as he struggled and screamed, his body shaking with rage. I wondered how such a little body could vibrate with so much strength and rage.

When Cale's anger and rage were finally spent, I was determined this would never happen again. My son would get the help he needed, one way or another. I carried Cale downstairs, out the door, and into my van, stopping only to grab my purse. I began the 45 minute trip back to emergency, feeling more alone and uncertain than I ever could remember, but also angry, frustrated and determined.

As luck would have it, the same doctor was on duty at emergency. When he entered the room both Cale and I were crying – Cale because he felt that he was a horrible child, and I because I was exhausted, and scared and very close to hopeless.

The doctor put his chart down and reached over and rubbed Cale's head. He then looked at me and said "What do you need me to do?"

His kindness and his willingness to listen to what we needed unlocked the flood gates, and I broke down. In between sobs I asked him to admit Cale to the hospital so that we could get some help. He agreed and Cale spent the next 11 days under the care of Dr. Smythe. Initially, however, he saw another pediatrician as Dr. Smythe was on vacation, and his medications were immediately adjusted. He was placed on the pediatric floor, and because there weren't any child psychiatry beds, per se, I or another adult had to stay with Cale at all times. Over the next 11 days, I left the hospital only to shower and change clothes, calling home whenever I could to update Brad on what was happening. I was lost, lonely and scared, but determined not to let Cale see my desperation.

Tests were started the first day and that night Cale finally nodded off to sleep, having been given medication to help sedate him. Despite the medication he held tight to my hand and would awaken the moment I tried to move. Finally he fell deep enough asleep that I was able to move. Sitting in the darkness with the glow and the beep of the monitors in the background, I felt a huge, heavy, suffocating weight descend upon me. My son looked like an angel in the bed, his eyes closed and his chest rising and falling, rising and falling. What if we could never figure out what was wrong? How could I ever help him? Adam was at home and I barely knew him because of all the time I spent trying to get help for Cale. Would Adam eventually hate me for not being there when he was growing up? How could this ever get straightened out? What had I done wrong? How could I fix it? How could I get my son, and my family, the help we so desperately needed? What was I missing?

I knelt beside Cale's bed and laid my head on the pillow beside his head and cried. Huge sobs exploded from my chest, wracking my body. I knew that I would probably wake Cale up, but I couldn't stop. The exhaustion, worry, lack of sleep and pain of watching my child suffer, along with missing my other child immensely, the tension in my relationship with Brad and the demands of work had taken its toll. I was empty. I had nothing left to give. I continued crying until I felt a soft touch on my shoulder. Looking up, I saw one of the nurses standing beside me. She sat down on the chair, hesitated for a moment, then spoke.

"You are the reason your son is not getting help," she said.

I stopped crying immediately. If she was trying to get my attention, she had succeeded. I fought the impulse to tell her to get lost, to be quiet, that she didn't know what she was talking about. Instead, I waited.

Seeing that I was willing to listen, she continued. She explained that because Cale had two loving, good parents who would not abandon him, he was not considered by the system to be 'a crisis' or 'in crisis'.

"He is in crisis in yours eyes, but not in the system's because they know you will keep taking him home, keep loving him and keep trying to help him," she said, adding so many other children with mental health issues had no stable home to return to, and were often in the care of the children's aid society.

Her advice was to refuse to take Cale home until appointments had been scheduled with all the appropriate people.

"And don't ever forget you know your son better than anyone else in this world," she said. It was a piece of advice I would forever cherish.

The next day when talk began of sending Cale home, I remembered my nighttime conversation with my nurse angel and stood firm, refusing to even consider taking Cale home until I had appointments slips in hand. Because Dr. Smythe was on vacation we had not even had the opportunity to see her yet.

The nurse's advice worked, and Cale remained in the hospital for more than a week, during which time he was seen by Dr. Smythe, and appointments were scheduled with social workers at a Southwestern Ontario children's mental health centre. Towards the end of Cale's stay, after he had been moved to a private room, Cale became agitated and wrapped a bed sheet around his neck. Before I knew what was happening I had been pushed out of the room and a 'code white' was called for Cale. Security officers, doctors and nurses rushed into the room. Dread filled my body and mind as I listened to Cale's screaming in agony, perhaps both emotional and physical, as he was restrained on the bed. I remember sliding down the wall to the floor and covering my ears to block out the sound. Surely this could not be happening! When I returned to the room, Cale had been given medication to calm him, and he lay on the bed, tears flowing silently from his eyes. As I walked towards his bed he turned his head away from me.

In the months that followed Cale was taken off Prozac and placed on Paxil which, after a brief period of improvement, lead to increased irritability, agitation and impulsivity. He was taken off Paxil and Buspar was added to his medication regimen. We began counseling, Cale alone and with Brad and I, with a social worker, **Aaron White at the children's mental health facility. We met with Dr. Marks in London for our prearranged appointment. An in-home worker from the same Southwestern Ontario children's mental health facility began visiting our home. His role was to help Brad and I figure out how to structure our home and deal with Cale. It was overwhelming and crazy and it felt like I was living in a fishbowl. But slowly it began to feel like things might be turning around.

We received Dr. Marks report in February 1998 and it confirmed much of what we had already suspected. Cale's symptoms, Dr. Marks said, were "reminiscent of ADHD but they may be consistent with his anxiety and mood difficulties."

She indicated she felt that Cale had a significant mood disorder that appeared to be cyclical in fashion but added she was reticent to label him as bipolar at that time. She added however, that he did have some features that seemed to be consistent with an early bipolar pattern.

Dr. Marks further recommended that Cale continue attending counseling at the children's mental health facility he was attending, undergo psychometric testing, and that a school conference be held to discuss the finding and recommendations of the psychometric testing.

She also acknowledged something I had been wrestling with for quite some time – the fact that it was highly likely that medications prescribed to me during my pregnancy with Cale might have adversely affected him.

As guilty as I felt about this, there was nothing I could do. I was not a perfect parent, and had never claimed to be. Instead, I concentrated, on learning from my mistakes and trying to do the best I could for my children. The medication I had taken while pregnant with Cale had been prescribed by specialists who assured me it would not harm my baby. These doctors were supposed to know, and I was supposed to be able to trust them. I had believed in their expertise, although I had doubted it since. Drowning in guilt now would do little to help Cale, so I focused on moving forward.

As suggested by Dr. Marks, Cale's pediatrician started him on Valproic Acid – a medication used for seizures which also had effective properties as a mood stabilizer. She suggested that Risperidone could be added if needed for anxiety.

Valproic Acid would be the first medication which Brad and I felt was helpful to Cale and which provided us with some hope. Within four weeks of starting the medication Cale became noticeably calmer and less irritable. He began to sleep better and he seemed happier. We saw his sense of humour return.

I began to get an idea of which behaviours were symptoms of his illness, which were simply part of his age, and which were, in fact, just behaviours. Some, I knew, had manifested themselves as a result of my over protectiveness and the inability to properly address issues because of the illness. So when Cale was accepted into a pre-adolescent program at the children's mental health facility, I was happy. Perhaps now we could not only provide Cale with the medical treatment he required, but also the the support and instruction he needed to learn how to integrate his mental illness into his life, distinguish between behaviour and symptoms and learn to help himself. Brad and I hoped we could also learn what we needed to know. The program offered comprehensive assessment and short-term treatment services to children six to 12 years of age. Through a structured environment and individualized treatment plans, children and their families, we learned, are helped to learn and develop adaptive behaviours and skills necessary for successful functioning in their homes, schools and communities.

Cale was part of an 8 am to 8 pm program, beginning March 17, 1988. This meant Cale would arrive at the on-site school each day for 8 a.m. After school he attended the second part of the program, in more of a home type setting. I was to pick him up each evening by 8 p.m. The program was set up in such a way that all attempts were made to avoid disrupting positive ties Cale had to us, his family, and the community. Brad and I were told from the beginning that a high level of parental involvement would be expected at both the assessment and treatment stages. We would also be expected to enroll in a series of parenting class facilitated by **Paul Storey, a child and youth worker at the facility, and his colleague. Storey was also head of Cale's team at the 8 to 8 program..

It sounded great to me. I was willing to do whatever I needed to do to help my family. I did not see the issue as Cale's problem. I saw it as something our entire family needed to deal with and learn from. Nor did I see it as behavioural, although I was aware that behavioural aspects had come to exist due to the day to day dealing of Cale's mental illness.

During the orientation Brad and I learned that the philosophy of the program was to offer a secure and understanding environment in which a child could work through his/her emotional/social/behavioural problems. It emphasized the development of adaptive behaviour through the use of positive feedback, rather than through attempts to extinguish inappropriate behaviour through punishment.

The program, we were told, worked with the entire family. Parents were not seen as 'bad' or 'inadequate' but instead received help to develop the skills needed to feel a sense of empowerment, a sense that they can be successful as parents. In order to be most successful parents needed to be open to examining their own beliefs and practices about parenting.

Before Cale began the program I spent a great deal of time talking to him about it. I didn't want him to feel that he was being punished. His father and I were involved and would be working hard as well. Having already formed a good relationship with Aaron White, our service coordinator, Cale seemed comfortable with this next step.

Aaron's role, as I saw it, was to coordinate Cale's assessment and treatment program, provide therapy and counseling to Cale and the rest of our family, communicate and consult with us in regard to Cale's program, and consult with other staff and community resources who were or may need to be involved.

Cale was assigned to a group of child and youth workers headed by Paul Storey, who was responsible for developing and implementing Cale's treatment plan.

While involved in the program Cale would attend the facility's school, which offered small classrooms, allowing for individualized programming geared towards promoting success, as well as affording the opportunity for close contact with the teacher.

As parents, Brad and I were expected to work with the team and transfer new skills and behaviours to our home and community via new behaviour management techniques and understanding. Behaviour management, we were told, generally involved natural and logical consequences. For example, if a child did not settle down at bedtime, he/she would be expected to go to bed earlier the following evening.

Natural and logical consequences, however, could not always be used. Children who deliberately damaged property might be required to work to pay off the damage. Physical aggression could result in various levels of 'grounding.'

Further, we learned, on occasions where a child lost his/her self control and caused physical injury to himself or others, or serious property damage, he/she could be physically restrained by the staff, in order to assist the child in regaining control. We were assured these physical interventions would last only as long as it took for the child to settle down, and would never involve mechanical restraints. All staff had undergone training in proper restraint techniques.

I listened to the information concerning restraints with great anxiety, but felt certain that these techniques would not be needed with Cale. Perhaps I was just being naïve, or I wanted so badly for us to get help that I was willing to push this point to the back of my mind. For whatever reason, I didn't worry about the issue of restraints.

Cale jumped into the program with both feet, as did I. Brad participated as much as his work schedule would allow, and Adam participated whenever our entire family was requested to attend. Whether at the program or in the parenting class, I listened to everything that was said and took extensive notes, determined to do whatever I could to help my family.

Cale seemed to respond well, on a general basis, and in particular formed a close bond with Paul and another Child and Youth Worker (CYW) named **James Black. Part of the program involved a communication book which traveled back and forth between the program and our home. Each morning I wrote notes about the previous evening and morning and each evening I received progress notes from the program.

For three months we worked hard to follow the program, but none of us harder than Cale. While Dr. Smythe worked with the facility nurse and ourselves to stabilize Cale's medication situation, the program team worked on anger management, communication and behaviour management. Strategies ranged from time outs and talking problems through, to the use of restraints – something I never in a million years would have considered. Faced, however, with Cale's escalating rage episodes, in which he would punch and kick walls, throw items like books, lamps and chairs, and his increasing size, it became an issue of safety – for Cale and those around him. We had been taught proper restraint techniques, and while I recognized the necessity, or thought I did, my heart broke each time it was necessary to use restraints. When the situation resolved and the crisis over, I would often retreat to my room, crying and praying for a different way; for something to change. In hindsight, it is my belief now that these episodes of rage were, in fact, symptoms of Cale's bipolar disorder and anxiety. I believe, now, that my child was restrained, both by program staff and his father and I, when what he needed from us with the proper medication, counselling and understanding and support. This is one area where I carry immense guilt and sadness. If I had the chance, this is what I would apologize to Cale for.

Despite this Cale made great strides during his stay at the program. Between his medication, which seemed to be working extremely well, and the techniques he had learned at the program, he was able to 'graduate' from the program. He returned to his school, near the end of Grade 6 – the month of June – and prepared to begin Grade 7.

Chapter Nine

The first few months of the next school year were relatively quiet for Cale in comparison to previous years. With his medication stabilized, he was able to handle most problems in a positive way, talking through disagreements and problem solving. Minor problems occurred, but they were much more easily solved than in the past. Cale and Adam continued to argue, but as brothers less than two years apart, it was nothing I didn't expect.

The school underwent a change of principals for Cale's seventh year and it didn't take me long to discover there might be problems. At that time I held the position of co-chair of the parent advisory committee at the school our school been one of the schools chosen to house a segregated 'behavioural' class and renovations were underway to prepare the room. Walls were being knocked out and new carpeting and flooring installed, amongst other things. During my first meeting with the new principal I was shocked to hear him refer to the students who might attend this class as 'those kids.' He went on to describe how it would be nice if the school board were willing to spend this kind of money on "the good kids too!"

Initially I assumed I had not heard properly, or had misunderstood. Seeking clarification I spoke to another parent, the PAC chairperson, who assured me she had understood the principal's comments in the same way. I was appalled and disappointed at his lack of professionalism and insensitivity. Worse, I worried about how he would treat Cale. I made an appointment to talk to him about the situation, and he assured me he had not meant to insinuate anything derogatory about the 'behavioural' students. I was not convinced.

Problems began to arise again and Cale began to wrack up suspensions in Grade 7 and 8. Where most of his past suspensions had been due to fighting, anger outbursts and refusing to do work, he no longer was suspended for these reasons. He had progressed – five days for cigarettes and lighter, 10 days for a pocket knife. He continued to struggle with academics, but was working hard to keep his anger under control.

One of the major issues Cale was dealing with at the time was he had become the target of daily teasing, taunting and harassment by two of his fellow students. On two occasions he was assaulted by one of these students, but did not fight back – an incredible achievement over incidents in the past in which Cale would have lost his temper and struck out in violence. The school refused to acknowledge this progress on Cale's part.

The other student continued to harass Cale, threatening on a daily basis to hurt, and even kill him. While Cale often responded verbally, he never became phsyical with the student, even though the situation continued for months. At one point the student described to Cale, quite vividly, how he planned to stab him to death with a pair of scissors. The threat was overheard by other students, who reported the incident to their parents and teachers. When I contacted the school to see what was being done about the situation, I learned that the student had been moved to a desk across the room from Cale, and moved to the front of the bus, which is where much of the harassment was taking place. Having been suspended for threats in the past, Cale questioned the double standard, and why he seemed to be treated so differently than other students by the school officials.

The situation with the other student, coupled with the difficulty Cale was experiencing academically began to affect Cale even more greatly. His anxiety level increased dramatically and I noticed a significant increase in what I called his 'stress' behaviours, such as cracking his knuckles and biting his fingers and nails. He also experienced an increase in physical illness, and I wondered if this was related to the stress he was feeling. He spent a period of about 2 ½ months sick with colds, flus and viruses, including 5th Disease, which never seemed to end. He also suffered from headaches, stomachaches and dizziness. Insomnia became a severe issue again, despite the medication he was on.

I noticed as well that Cale was beginning to worry excessively over things he had no control over or that were highly unlikely. When he heard a local radio station refer to an upcoming lunar eclipse as Armageddon, he became worried that it would, indeed, be the end of the world. I had to convince him that it was just a joke the radio station had started.

Everything came to a head for Cale halfway through Grade 8. During the first half of Grade 8 Cale was taught by a wonderful woman whom he enjoyed, and who seemed to have a knack for identifying and encouraging his strengths and talents. There were a few such teachers in his school. When his Grade 8 teacher left on maternity leave in December, she was replaced by a male teacher, *Mr. Duncan who also taught computer class and whom Cale had always been uncomfortable with. Cale felt Mr. Duncan did not like him, and he often felt centred out and belittled by the teacher's words and actions. Despite this Cale kept his temper and attempted to treat him with respect.

After missing over a week of school due to illness, Cale returned to school planning to ask Mr. Duncan for his missed assignments. We had discussed the issue before Cale headed to school. Often Cale would fail assignments he missed because he was not comfortable getting missed assignments from his fellow students. I encouraged Cale to go directly to his teacher for the assignments.

Cale asked Mr. Duncan for the missed assignments four times, and on four occasions he was told to get the assignments from another student. Cale continued to try to explain that he would prefer to get the assignment from Mr. Duncan.

Mr. Duncan finally gave Cale a copy of someone else's assignment to copy, but did not explain it. Before Cale had a chance to finish copying the assignment Mr. Duncan took it away, returning it to its owner.

Cale remained confused and at the end of the class approached the teacher to explain his need for assistance. Mr. Duncan began yelling at Cale, who was also getting frustrated. Cale turned to walk away and Mr. Duncan grabbed him by the shirt, refusing to let him go and telling Cale to "never walk away from me."

Cale asked Mr. Duncan to let him go, then tried to pull away. Angry that Mr. Duncan would not let go, Cale swore at him and was sent to the office.

At the office the principal refused to allow Cale to explain his side of the story or defend his actions. Angry and more frustrated, Cale swore at the principal and received a three-day suspension. I would later talk to both the principal and Mr. Duncan, along with students who witnessed the incident, and all agreed with Cale's version of the situation.

Cale came home angry and confused about the double-standards being used at the school. While he admitted he was wrong to swear, he felt Mr. Duncan had purposely antagonized him. He felt Mr. Duncan had no right to grab him by the shirt.

I was furious. There was no doubt in my mind that Mr. Duncan had assaulted Cale by grabbing his shirt and refusing to let go. Worse, he had antagonized, demeaned and belittled him unnecessarily. I repeatedly ran into roadblocks trying to talk to the teacher and the principal about the situation. We received 'official' notice of the suspension seven days after the incident. It included a clause saying if we chose to appeal, the appeal must be filed within 7 days of the incident.

Cale was devastated, angry, hurt, confused, and once again emotionally broken. One more time the school system had shown him that he didn't matter; that those in authority, and even other students, did not have to follow the same rules as him.

Cale did not return to school after the suspension, and I forwarded a letter to the board superintendent concerning the situation. She called to express 'how therapeutic' it must have been for me to write the letter, and said there was nothing that could be done. For me, her phone call was the proverbial straw that broke the camel's back. Cale left the school permanently

We began researching other alternatives for Cale's education. Although it meant driving Cale to and from Windsor each day, about a 45-minute drive each way, we decided to enroll him in a private Christian school there for the remainder of Grade 8. I shared the driving responsibilities with another family. I soon came to wish I had made the move sooner, for both of my boys. Cale was welcomed with open arms at the private school, and did well in the smaller classrooms with more one-on-one attention. The first time I was paged by the school, I remember dialing frantically, worried that something terrible had happened. I was so used to being paged on an almost daily basis, that I expected nothing less. Sensitive to my concerns, the principal's first words were "there's no emergency; nothing is wrong." She had called instead to tell me what a good day Cale had had.

Later, when plans were being finalized for a week-long field trip to Muskoka Woods, I would be surprised to learn I was not expected to chaperone. In fact, I was not wanted. In the past it had been demanded that I attend most field trips so that I could 'handle' Cale. The Muskoka trip was one of the best experiences of Cale's school life. Once home he talked about it for days. At the end of the year Cale graduated with the students at this private school who had quickly become his friends.

As Cale entered high school Brad and I observed another shift taking place and began to wonder whether his medication was becoming less effective. Perhaps adolescence and the onset of puberty and change in hormonal levels were affecting the way the medication worked. I still don't know.

What I do know is Cale began once again to experience severe anxiety, stress, insomnia, and episodes of rage. Adding to Cale, and Adam's, anxiety was the fact that Brad and I separated for about 10 months beginning in the summer of 2000. The separation was my decision, and my hope was that it would force Brad and I to make the time to communicate with each other and work things out. Eventually that did happen, but the separation was very difficult for both of the boys. For my part, I was emotionally exhausted.

By the time Brad and I reunited in March 2001, and I moved home from the apartment I had rented, Cale's anxiety was quite apparent. I hoped that as things settled down at home, he would stabilize.

The next two years, until shortly before his death, would be a roller coaster ride of highs and lows, twists and turns, brought on by the Bipolar Disorder. In the summer of 2001 we headed to Northern Ontario, where we had rented a cottage, for vacation. Ange was accompanying us, along with one of Cale's friends with whom he had quite a volatile relationship. It was a wrong decision on my part, agreeing to allow the young man to come with us. Hindsight is a wonderful thing.

Once at our destination, Lake Commanda, the tension and issues which erupted between Cale and his friend, along with the excitement of being on vacation and the change – set Cale on edge. I learned later that the excitement of an upcoming event or holiday, and the anxiety of dealing with that same situation, can be very difficult for persons with mental illness. On this particular vacation Cale's anger flared and his friend antagonized. Recognizing that he was quickly heading for a full blown rage episode, I brought him to the emergency room at North Bay's hospital. There I was told by the attending physician that I could probably do a better job of adjusting Cale's medication to get him through the week than he could! With that we were sent on our way. That was when I realized how very little the medical community really knew about child and adolescent mental illness.

Cale wisely decided to take care of himself for the next week, recognizing what he needed. Leaving his friend to hang out with Adam and Ange, Cale spent much of his time by himself in the boat, fishing and enjoying the lake. As always this had a calming effect on him and he was able to enjoy his vacation.

We enjoyed a particularly fun afternoon one day when I made a comment about wishing I could bring home some large rocks from the lake to place by our pond. Cale and his friend worked together to dig up the rocks I identified, each one a little bigger than the last. They then dragged the rocks up the hill to the cottage. One of the larger rocks now sits by our pond. Another sits by Peggy and John's pond.

The night in North Bay was the first of many trips to emergency which Cale and I would make in a relatively short period of time. Over the next 18 months or so, Cale's anxiety, stress and episodes of rage continued. Academics continued to cause problems at school, and he continued to struggle with acceptance and fitting in. We continued to work with his pediatrician to find the right medications for him. Where Valproic Acid had worked in the past, it seemed to have lost its effect.

Of most concern to me, however, was Cale's increasingly more frequent comments concerning death and not wanting to live. On three occasions he was admitted to an adolescent mental health facility in Southwestern Ontario because of the threat of self harm and the need for medical stabilization. This facility was the only place where older youth and families could access the only child psychiatrist serving our community. That psychiatrist worked only half time. Joanne visited Cale one day while he was there, bringing him lunch from Burger King and just talking to him. Cale had just come out of a very bad relationship with a young lady he thought he was in love with. Joanne was astounded to hear Cale say he felt no one would ever love him...that he was unlovable.

"He truly, truly believed it," she told me later. It broke her heart to know a 15-year-old boy believed himself to be so unlovable that he did not want to live.

In the following months Cale struggled with alcohol abuse and drug experimentation, issues with his girlfriend, problems with school, isolation and despair. He talked to me about most of these things, but it seemed they were out of control and he was spiraling downward very, very quickly. I felt like I was spending most of my life on the phone trying to get help, trying to find answers. The rest of the time I was fighting to stay connected to my child, who was pulling away from me and the rest of our family, quickly and furiously.

It was just a few months before his death that Cale and I made his final trip to emergency. Although he did not want to be re-admitted to the adolescent mental health facility, Cale knew he would be safe there, so he asked me to take him back.

Agitated and angry, Cale jumped from my vehicle as I was heading towards the hospital. Terrified, I called the police. By the time they arrived at the hospital parking lot Cale was standing outside the car talking to me, anxious, terrified and agitated. He agreed to go into emergency when the police offered to escort us in so that we could be seen by a doctor quicker. After three hours they left, apologizing because we hadn't yet been seen. I spent those three hours, and another five or six sitting in a crowded emergency room with my son, a 16-year-old, 180 pound suicidal youth. Cale paced, back and forth, traveling an emotional road between deep depression and thoughts of suicide, and wondering why he needed to be at the hospital. After being taken into a room in emergency, it would be another seven hours before Cale was re-admitted to the adolescent mental health facility.

While there Cale's medication was adjusted again, and it was decided a trial with Lithium was advisable. Within weeks the Lithium showed signs of working for Cale, and easing his symptoms. Soon, he was better than I had seen him for a long, long time. He seemed calmer, happier. His sense of humour had returned. He was emotionally much stronger, strong enough to take his life.

After Cale's death I would read that many people who have struggled with depression and bipolar disorder for lengthy periods of time, and are placed on medication which ultimately works, are able to complete suicide. The theory is that the medication makes them feel better and provides them with the energy they need to carry out and complete the suicidal actions.

At the time, I simply couldn't understand why Cale would choose to follow through on his thoughts of suicide when he was finally beginning to feel better. Perhaps he said it best himself just a few weeks after starting Lithium. In the course of a conversation one evening, Cale told me he realized how sick he really was, by how good he was feeling on the Lithium. He also told me how sad that made him feel, knowing that he would need to continue taking this medication for the rest of his life if he wanted to feel 'normal.'

More than anything, Cale did not want to be sick.

Chapter Ten

Much too often the real Cale was overshadowed by what he did, or didn't do because of his mental illness. But there were many moments, hours, days if we were lucky – a lifetime of them - when Cale's disease seemed to take a vacation and we were left with a funny, intelligent, caring, compassionate, life loving young man. At these times he approached life with exuberance and an off center sense of humour that often brought me to tears.

They say a picture paints a thousand words. If that is so, then my mind is filled with thousands and thousands, hundreds of thousands of words, for my mind is filled with pictures.

One of the few times Cale was truly content as an infant was when he was breastfeeding. It was then that this fussy, agitated baby would latch onto my breast, the furrows in his forehead would smooth out and his tiny fists would relax. I would stroke his blonde hair, his head and cheeks, or hold his hand as he nursed. Even then, at that young age, I wondered what was going on inside this tiny body. But for the period of time that he nursed, I gloried in the bond between us, his relaxation and peacefulness causing the same response in me.

Cale was christened in March of 1997, wearing an outfit I had made for him, and a full length eyelet jacket I had made for Adam's christening.

We were joined at the altar by his Godparents, Tim Stiers and his Aunt Brenda. He looked like an angel, his blond hair shining like a halo.

When Cale was about two years old Brad and I were standing in the back yard of Brad's parents home talking with them, Judy and John and Brenda and Keith. Adam and Cale were in the yard with us. We suddenly noticed that we could not see Cale, and something drew my gaze to the barn. Cale had often been in Grampa's barn with others, and I just wondered if he might have decided to go in on his own. Heading to the barn we soon realized that Cale had not only entered the large structure, but had climbed a ladder into the second floor hay loft. Seeing us, he started giggling. Brad headed up the ladder slowly, not wanting to turn the situation into a game or adventure for Cale, who stood dangerously close to gaps and holes in the hay loft floor big enough for him to slip through. Thankfully Brad was able to reach Cale, and brought him down, grinning from ear to ear.

Snapshots run through my mind. Brad, Adam, Cale and I fishing from a boat on Eagle Lake is South River, silhouetted again the setting sun. Cale and Brad were at the front of the boat, and I took a picture of them, father and son, back to back, each fishing off the opposite side, each focused on the chore at hand. The picture oozes peacefulness and serenity and an incredible bond between father and son. Eating lunch with Margaret Stiers and her children, when she made pancakes in the shape of the first initial of each child's name. For months afterwards, Cale wouldn't settle for anything but a pancake in the shape of a 'C'. Swimming with Adam and Cale at Point Pelee and standing in the surf holding hands while four-foot waves crashed into us. Sitting on the back porch watching as a huge moth emerged from a cocoon.

A picture sits on the desk upstairs, of Adam, Cale and Shadow, a black Spaniel-mix dog we had at the time. The boys are probably around eight and 10 or nine and 11 years old. The picture shows them sitting on rocks in a river, casting stones into the water, the dog at their side. The picture captures a peaceful, serene event. The boys and I, along with Shadow, had driven to Tennessee to visit my sister Ghislaine, and my brother-in-law Jim, who owned a campground in Crossville. It was a relaxing, wonderful trip with lots of sightseeing and plenty of time spent together. Adam, Cale and I left one day early and headed into

Gatlinburg and the Smoky Mountains. It was there, near the entrance to the Smoky Mountain National Park that we stopped by the river and the picture was taken.

On the way home, exhausted at 3 a.m. we decided to pull into a Motel 6 in Ohio. While checking in we learned that only small dogs were allowed to stay. We assured the clerk that Shadow, who was definitely a medium size dog, was small and quiet. With the room paid for, Adam, Cale and I snuck Shadow into the room, shielding him from the clerk's view with our bodies. As Shadow was not much of a barker, we were sure that getting him into the room would be the hardest part. Once in the room, the three of us collapsed in laughter.

The next morning we left the room intending to sneak Shadow out a side or back door. Little did we know that a cleaning lady stood in the hallway, waiting, or so it seemed, to foil our plans. One look at Shadow and she was in love, proclaiming in a loud voice what a beautiful dog he was, and urging her fellow workers to come and see her. Eyes wide, the boys and I just looked at one another, trying hard not to burst into laughter. The clerk never did say anything, and we headed for home laughing about the situation. Cale and Adam enjoyed telling their father about our escapades later.

As toddlers, Adam and Cale used to play outside with Shadow, often burying the patient dog in leaves. When it snowed, the boys, bundled up in snowsuits, boots, hats and mittens, would head outside to play. Often Shadow would run up from behind, grab the boys' hats from the top of their heads and run away. Cale's initial anger would dissipate into giggles as Shadow raced around the yard, a hat in his mouth.

Even as a toddler Cale was quite rambunctious and I often wonder, to this day, how he managed not to break any bones. Trying to fly by jumping out of a large bush in our front yard earned Cale a trip to the hospital with what we worried was a broken cheek bone. There were no broken bones, but between the black eye and the swollen cheek, for days I was afraid to take him anywhere for fear that someone would think I had hit him.

Swinging from the pole in his closet earned him another trip to the hospital. However, because he had split his toe where it met his foot, nothing could be done except to tape it up.

On a trip to Niagara Falls when the boys were quite young, probably around five and seven-years-old, we had the incredible pleasure of camping beside a middle-aged couple from Pennsylvania who we soon began to refer to as *Gramma and Grampa Butler. They fell in love with Cale and Adam, and for the rest of the vacation, when we weren't off sight seeing, we were trying to get the boys to come back to our camper and leave Gramma and Grampa alone. The Butlers however, enjoyed the boys, spoiling them rotten during the time we were there, and buying them each a stuffed animal to take home. For years after that summer we corresponded with them, exchanging pictures, audio tapes, cards and letters.

Cale and Adam went through a phase when they enjoyed skateboarding, and would practice moves on the back steps for hours and hours. The noise drove me crazy, and the bumps, bruises, cuts and scrapes scared me to death, but I admired their tenacity and determination to learn.

During their years in elementary school Adam, Cale and I developed a Friday morning routine of going to Burger King for breakfast. We were there often enough that the woman working the counter memorized what each of us liked and would place our order as we entered the restaurant. These mornings were filled with conversation, trickery (as the boys attempted to shoot their straw papers at me without me seeing them in time to stop them), and humour. Usually at least one or two of their teachers would gather for breakfast as well. Depending on who it was, the boys would choose either the furthest table away, or a table very close by. Fridays were the easiest day of the week for me to get the boys out of bed and ready to go out the door.

Cale had gotten his beginner's drivers licence the November before he died, so for the months that followed he wanted to drive everywhere. I soon learned that he tended to have a heavy foot, like his mom. He seemed to learn quickly, however, and was soon driving as much as I.

After his death, we sold the van to a close friend. It was too hard for me to drive because of my back injury, and also because of the pain in my heart. Everytime I got into the van I expected to hear Cale saying "Can I drive, Mom?"

The winter before his death, Cale was visiting friends in Belle River while I was visiting my sister Joanne, about ten minutes away. We had made arrangements for Cale to get a ride from a friend and be dropped off at Joanne's house a little later.

Joanne and I were talking when the front door of her house flew open and Cale burst in, his cheeks red and grinning from ear to ear. He was barefoot, in the middle of winter, and holding his shoes in his hand. He quickly began telling Joanne and I how he and a friend had been jumping from the road into huge snowdrifts along the banks of the river in town. His booming voice filled the room as he described jumping and hitting the snow banks, the momentum carrying them down in a tumble of arms and legs. He was soaked from head to foot and of course his shoes and socks were soaked. But his happiness filled the room, and our hearts.

When the boys were young I painted several shelves bright red to put in their room. I then encouraged Adam and Cale to dip their hands in white paint and place handprints all over the shelves. I joined in. I still have the shelves, covered in my sons' handprints. They will belong to Adam's children someday.

In the summer of 2002 we attended a family reunion. Cale, John, Ange and I spent most of the day in the pool, horsing around, playing volleyball and just having a good time. It is another of those memories I am so thankful for.

That same summer Brad and I bought tickets to take Adam, Ange and Cale to see David Lee Roth and Sammy Hagar live at a concert at DTE in Detroit. Adam and Ange were unable to attend so Cale, Brad and I went. It was an incredible evening, and we were on our feet singing and dancing the entire night. Cale loved the concert and talked about it all the way home.

Cale also loved Harleys and had amassed books, blankets, hats and other Harley paraphernalia over the years. I was terrified of motorcycles, having lost my younger brother in a motorcycle accident. I knew, however, that it was only a matter of time before Cale began riding bikes, and I knew I would have to get used to the idea. Cale, however, respected my concern and never brought up his desire to buy a Harley some day. After he died, Brad and I packed up all his Harley blankets and pillows to pass on to his niece or nephew some day.

There are many, many more memories and good times – holiday celebrations at Gramma Dolan's and Gramma and Grampa Simon's, eating frozen creampuffs at Gramma Simon's, vacations at the cabin in South River, coming out of the lake covered in leeches in Kirkland Lake, traveling to British Columbia, rescuing animals, reading story books in bed, visiting Colleen, Uncle Joe and Aunt Mary in Wallaceburg; going for breakfast, just me and the three kids so Uncle Joe, Aunt Mary and Brad could sleep in, handmade birthday and Mother's Day cards, getting hooked on Mario Brothers and Judge Dredd and sneaking in (and getting caught) to play after the boys fell asleep, learning RAP songs and listening to the words of Marilyn Manson songs because Cale wanted me to 'hear the message', arguing over Coke versus Pepsi, and Bob Seger's version of Turn the Page versus Gun's n' Roses' version, working on projects, watching Brad and Cale work on separate projects together in the shop, listening to Adam, Ange and Cale talking on the back steps, trampoline talks, driving the dune buggy Brad had built, riding the dirt bike, ice cream at the Dairy Freez, camping at Jellystone and Wheatley Provincial Park, bonfires...while camping and at home in our back yard, roasting hotdogs and marshmallows and making pie irons...

The day before he died, Cale was laying on the couch watching a comedy special on television. It was a stand up act by comedian John Leguizamo. Brad and I were seated a few feet away, at the dining room table working on our income tax return. Cale howled with laughter at Leguizamo's words and antics, and repeatedly turned to Brad and I to ask if we had seen the last part. While we were sort of paying attention to the show, Brad and I were finding more humour in watching Cale and listening to him roar with laughter. His laughter was contagious and we found ourselves laughing with him.

It was a relaxed, carefree, fun afternoon that all three of us enjoyed in the moment. I don't believe I could have enjoyed it more even if I had known Cale's life would end the next day. It is another gift that I will cherish for all time – the chance to have laughed so freely and experienced such joy with my child before he died.

Epilogue

God chose me to be mother to both Cale and Adam. This is the greatest gift I have ever been given in my life.

I was not a perfect mother. I made many mistakes and continue to make mistakes. This is how I grow in the roles I am supposed to fill – by making mistakes and learning from them.

I believe there is a reason that I was chosen to be the mother of these incredible young men, Adam and Cale. I don't believe it was random for either one.

In Cale's case, for some reason, I had the ability to see that his difficulties were far beyond the 'normal', and had more than just a partial basis in mental health issues. God gave me the ability to forge a wonderful bond with my child that allowed him to talk to me freely and safely. For this I will always be grateful. It was through this communication that Cale helped me to understand the world of mental illness from his point of view, and probably the point of view of many other youth. I learned an incredible amount, and received a lifetime of gifts, from my experience as Cale's mother.

Brad too, learned a great deal. While I can't speak for him, I can speak about what I witnessed. In the last years of Cale's life, despite his fear,

Brad struggled hard to understand his son's illness, and to forge a stronger, more open and loving relationship with him. He tried very hard to be there for Cale and to find ways to spend time with him and share with him. Cale admired his father and loved him. Brad admired his son's gifts, was learning to understand his illness, and loved him.

Another of the greatest gifts I see from Cale's death is Brad's relationship with Adam. Brad is loving and open with our oldest son, and more importantly, is available to him. They often share a beer and long conversations in Brad's garage, and Brad encourages Adam to talk about Cale, although Adam still chooses mainly to keep this part of his life private. Their relationship is more mature, more solid. Brad knows how short and tenuous life can be. I see him trying to make the most of his relationship with Adam. Brad admires and loves Adam.

For my part I watch Brad with admiration, knowing how very hard he has worked to become a good father and husband. I have never seen a man change so much, in such positive ways. I admire and love him.

Cale is gone, but my work has not ended. I promised Cale I would continue to fight for increased awareness, acceptance, tolerance and assistance for children and youth with mental health difficulties. I intend to keep this promise, and take it further. I will work for change for all people with mental illness, not just children and youth, for it made absolute sense to me that children and youth with mental illness become adults with mental illness.

I have received so many gifts from Cale…in his lifetime and since he chose to leave this life…too many to count. Cale taught me what it is to be a mother…and a human being. He taught me about unconditional love and accepting people for who they are, even if I, or others, perceive them to be different. Cale taught me the importance of looking past the 'package', of not prejudging and of giving people a chance. He taught me that sometimes people need help….like the snapping turtle who had lost his way and was wandering a dangerous highway. He taught me that sometimes people just need to be supported and believed in…like when Cale decided he wanted to be a counselor and work with troubled youth. He taught me, through this same situation, how easily and quickly a person's dreams can be destroyed.

Cale taught me that I could make a difference for people…like when Cale brought a friend home to visit – a friend who was afraid to meet me because, as Cale told me, "mothers never like him because of his piercings and coloured hair." Cale told his friend 'his' mom didn't care about things like that. What Cale didn't know was that he taught me not to care about things like that. In his lifetime, Cale taught me about loving people the way he wanted so desperately to be loved and accepted.

Cale also taught me about loyalty and friendship. Cale was a big fan of NASCAR driver Kyle Petty. It didn't matter that Kyle was not the greatest of drivers, and in fact rarely won a race that Cale watched. It didn't matter that other people teased him about liking Kyle. Cale told me he liked that Kyle was a family man and organized a charity cross-county motorcycle event every year to raise money for sick children. Despite teasing from other NASCAR fans, Cale refused to switch allegiance to a more successful driver. Kyle Petty was it.

With his death, and in the years that have followed, Cale continues to bring me gifts and lessons. Early on I made a promise to celebrate Cale and look for the gifts in his life and death, rather than choosing to remain in constant mourning. Cale has given me the gift of knowing that this is a decision I must make every day, even though it is not always easy. In fact, sometimes it is easier to choose to be angry, mean and miserable. There are many days when I forget to make the decision to look for the good; to be open for the gifts. When I realize this, I mourn the time lost, because it is time when I could have been open to the gifts. There are days it simply hurts too much; when I am in so much emotional and physical pain from missing Cale…but there is always the decision to be made – to stay in the pain or move forward.

Cale has taught me that life is too short to be angry and carry grudges. He has taught me that I can talk about his life, death, and his suicide, even if people don't always want to hear it. My experiences can help others, just as those of others have helped me in my healing. Cale has also taught me that his experience can help others. I often am asked to speak about my situation and Cale's death and it is rare that tears don't flow in the audience. Almost always, someone comes to talk to me afterwards, often to tell me of a similar story involving a loved one.

Often the story has been held secret for many, many years, or is talked of only in certain situations because of the stigma attached to suicide. Cale's death has taught me there should be no stigma, and that perhaps if the stigma that surrounds mental illness did not exist, fewer people would turn to suicide as a final way to end the pain.

In his death Cale has taught me that there is no timetable for healing; that no matter how hard you work or what you do to help you forget and heal, the pain of grief and loss exists, and must be dealt with. It's not always better after the first year... and to this day I don't believe it gets easier with time. It gets different. Cale has taught me that on the easiest days, and on the very hardest of days, if I pray, God listens. Perhaps it is the act of prayer itself, I'm not sure. I just know when I pray, my pain eases. It's that simple.

Most of all, Cale has taught me that all I have to do is believe and be ready, and he is with me. He is never far from me, but it is during those times that I am most lost in grief that he seems to be the farthest. I believe that my grief creates a barrier around me that he cannot penetrate.

When I am open he is there...it is that simple. Just before Christmas 2004 I woke up one morning at about 3 a.m. with the following poem running through my mind. The words flowed as if Cale were speaking to, and through me. I got up and began typing them into the computer.

When the poem was completed, I shared it with the other members of my suicide survivors support group. The following May I read it at the 13th Annual CMHA (Windsor Essex) Suicide Vigil.

Thank you, Cale, for this and all your gifts. I love you and I am with you always.

I Am With You Always

Be open. Be ready. Believe. I am with you always.

Feel me in the gentle breeze lifting your hair; caressing your face.

See me when the sun suddenly bursts through the clouds following the rain
and fingers of brilliant light slant towards the earth.

When a red flash flickers before you, the telltale song of the cardinal fills the air;
when dew diamonds dance across the delicate strands of a spider web;
when your breath swirls, warm against the cold of a crisp winter day...
trust that I am with you.

In dark moments, when you whisper my name; cry out for my presence.

Believe. Be still; quiet your thoughts.

I live in the flutter of your heart and the silence of the night;
in the craziness of work and the joy of play
in the serenity of prayer and the peace of reflection;
in your fear, sorrow, loss, anger and isolation...I live.

When you need me most yet feel me least;
time passes much too swiftly, yet minutes hang like hours;
the normal routine of your day becomes tedious, tears come unbidden
and the pain of sorrow seeps into your soul – I am with you.

I am the joy of a young child's giggle; the wisdom of an old man's words;
the smile of a stranger and the comfort of a friend's embrace.

I smile with you when an unexpected phone call brings good news
and dreaded occasions bring surprising peace rather than sorrow.

I am the vibration in the crashing thunder of a spring storm
and the warmth of the summer sun upon your face.

I am the crunching of autumn leaves and the howling of the winter wind.

On special days, and everyday; at common occasions and extraordinary events;
during unexpected moments; in thoughts that pass in a split second;
when reason make no sense and words have no meaning...I am with you.

I shine my light when sadness is an overwhelming shroud;
the unforgiving grip of fear is tight around your heart;
when the simple act of breathing becomes complex
and each moment of living is a conscious choice.

I celebrate with you when moments of unexpected joy explode in front of you,
and the inherent goodness of humankind warms your soul.

I rest with you in peace and strengthen you as each new day is born.

Don't wait for a certain moment or special time, for you may miss me.
I have no set schedule, no special place, no favourite season.
I am with you. It is that simple.
At all times and in all places; in your every breath and thought.
In every song you sing, every tear you cry; in laughter, joy, anger, sorrow.
In your dreams and your awakenings.
I am with you always.
Just believe.

Diane Simon – December 15, 2004

Facts On Depression & Bipolar Disorder In Children & Youth

Bipolar disorder (manic-depressive illness) affects numerous children and adolescents. Abrupt swings of mood and energy that occur multiple times within a day, intense outbursts of temper, poor frustration tolerance, and oppositional defiant behaviors are commonplace in juvenile-onset bipolar disorder. These children veer from irritable, easily annoyed, angry mood states to silly, goofy, giddy elation, and then just as easily descend into low energy periods of intense boredom, depression and social withdrawal, fraught with self-recriminations and suicidal thoughts. Recent studies have found that from the time of initial manifestation of symptoms, it takes an average of ten years before a diagnosis is made.

Bipolar disorder--manic-depression--was once thought to be rare in children. Now researchers are discovering that not only can bipolar disorder begin very early in life, it is much more common than ever imagined. **Yet the illness is often misdiagnosed or overlooked.** Why? Bipolar disorder manifests itself **differently in children than in adults,** and in children there is an overlap of symptoms with other childhood psychiatric disorder. As a result, these children may be given any number of psychiatric labels: **"ADHD," "Depressed," "Oppositional Defiant Disorder," "Obsessive Compulsive Disorder," or "Separation Anxiety Disorder."** Too often they are treated with stimulants or antidepressants--medications which can actually worsen the bipolar condition. The following are some frequently asked questions about childhood bipolar disorder, answered by Dr. Demitri Papolos and his wife, Janice, the authors of the book, *The Bipolar Child - The Definitive and Reassuring Guide to Childhood's Most Misunderstood Disorder.*

What is early-onset bipolar disorder and why are we suddenly hearing so much about it?

Early-onset bipolar disorder is manic-depression that appears early--very early--in life. For many years it was assumed that children could not suffer the mood swings of mania or depression, but researchers are now reporting that bipolar disorder (or early temperamental features of it) can occur in very young children, and that it is much more common that previously thought.

Is bipolar disorder in children the same thing as bipolar disorder in adults?

Adults seem to experience abnormally intense moods for weeks or months at a time, but children appear to experience such rapid shifts of mood that they commonly cycle many times within the day. This cycling pattern is called ultra-ultra rapid or ultradian cycling and it is most often associated with low arousal states in the mornings (these children find it almost impossible to get up in the morning) followed by afternoons and evenings of increased energy.

It is not uncommon for the first episode of early-onset disorder to be a depressive one. But as clinical investigators have followed the course of the disorder in children, they have reported a significant rate of transition from depression into bipolar mood states.

What are the symptoms in childhood, and how early can they begin?

We have interviewed many parents who report that their children seemed different from birth, or that they noticed that something was wrong as early as 18 months. Their babies were often extremely difficult to settle, rarely slept, experienced separation anxiety, and seemed overly responsive to sensory stimulation.

In early childhood, the youngster may appear hyperactive, inattentive, fidgety, easily frustrated and prone to terrible temper tantrums (especially if the word "no" appears in the parental vocabulary). These explosions can go on for prolonged periods of time and the child can become quite aggressive or even violent. (Rarely does the child show this side to the outside world.)

A child with bipolar disorder may be bossy, overbearing, extremely oppositional, and have difficulty making transitions. His or her mood can veer from morbid and hopeless to silly, giddy and goofy within very short periods of time. Some children experience social phobia, while others are extremely charismatic and risk-taking.

Symptoms of Mania:

- excessive energy, activity, restlessness, racing thoughts and rapid talking
- denial that anything is wrong
- extreme high or euphoric feeling
- easily irritated or distracted
- decreased need for sleep
- unrealistic beliefs in one's own ability and powers
- uncharacteristically poor judgment
- sustained period of behaviour that is different from usual
- unusual sexual drive
- abuse of drugs, particularly cocaine, alcohol or sleeping medications
- provocative, intrusive or aggressive behaviour

Symptoms of Depression:

- persistent sad, anxious or empty mood

- sleeping too much or too little; middle-of-the-night or early morning waking

- reduced appetite and weight loss or increased appetite and weight gain

- irritability or restlessness

- difficulty concentrating, remembering or making decisions

- fatigue or loss of energy

- persistent phsycial problems that don't respond to treatment

- thoughts of death or suicide, including suicide attempts

- feeling guilty, hopeless or worthless.

Summary Of Schizophrenia In Children

Schizophrenia is rare in children, but does occur. It affects about 1 in 40,000 compared to 1 in 100 adults. The average age of onset is 18 in men and 25 in women.

Children with schizophrenia experience difficulty managing everyday life. They share with their adult counter parts hallucinations, delusions, social withdrawal, flattened emotions, increased risk of suicide and loss of social and personal care skills. They may also share some symptoms with, and be mistaken for, children who suffer from autism or other pervasive development disabilities, which affect about 1 in 500 children. Although children with schizophrenia tend to be harder to treat and have a worse prognosis than adult-onset schizophrenia patients, researchers are finding that many children with schizophrenia can be helped by the new generation of anti-psychotic medications.

Childhood Schizophrenia and Bipolar Disorder Foundation; www.schizophrenia.com

Resources - Books

Acquainted with the Night: A Parent's Quest to Understand Depression and Bipolar Disorder in his Children; by Paul Raeburn.

How to Really Love Your Angry Child; by Ross Campbell

The Bipolar Child: The Definitive and Reassuring Guide to Childhood's Most Misunderstood Disorder; by Demitri F. Papolos and Janice Papolos

Misdiagnosis and Dual Diagnosis of Gifted Children and Adults: ADHD, Bipolar, OCD, Asperger's Syndrome and Other Disorders; by Edward Amend, Nadia Webb and Jean Goerss

Survival Strategies for Parenting Children with Bipolar Disorder; by George T. Lynn

How I Stayed Alive When My Brain was Trying to Kill Me: One Person's Guide to Suicide Prevention; by Susan Rose Blauner

When Life Hurts; by Phillip Yancey

When the Bough Breaks – Forever After the Death of a Son or Daughter; by Judith R. Bernstein

Sanity and Grace – A Journey of Suicide, Survival and Grace; by Judy Collins

Grieving Mental Illness; by Virginia Lafond

The Bipolar Disorder Survival Guide; by David Milkowitz

The Last Taboo; by Scott Simmie

Mental Illness for Women; by Rita Baron Faust

My Son, My Son – A Guide to Healing After Death, Loss, Suicide; by Iris Bolton

Night Falls Fast; by Kay Redfield Jamison

An Unquiet Mind; by Kay Redfield Jamison

The Suicide of My Son – A Story of Childhood Depression; by Trudy Carlson

Andrew, You Died Too Soon; by Corinne Chilstrom

Suicide – The Forever Decision; by Paul G. Quinnett

Living When a Loved One had Died; by Earl A. Grollman

Resources – Agencies And Organizations

Canada

Canadian Association for Suicide Prevention

c/o The Support Network
#301 – 11456 Jasper Avenue
Edmonton, Alberta. T5K 0M1
Tel: 780-482-0198; Fax: 780-488-1495
www.suicideprevention.ca
casp@suicideprevention.ca

Canadian Mental Health Association

8 King Street East, Suite 810
Toronto ON
M5C 1B5
Tel: 416-484-7750; Fax: 416-484-4617
www.cmha.ca; Emai: info@cmha.ca

Children's Mental Health Ontario —Sante Mentale pour Enfants Ontario

40 St. Clair Avenue East, Suite 309
Toronto, ON
N4T 1M9
Tel: 416-921-2109; 800-969-NMHA; Fax: 416-921-7600
www.cmho.org Email: info@cmho.org

Parents for Children's Mental Health Ontario

c/o 40 St. Clair Avenue East, Suite 309
Toronto, ON
M4T 1M9
Tel: 416-921-2109; Fax: 419-921-7600
www.parentsforchildrensmentalhealth.org;
Email: parents@parentsforchildrensmentalhealth.org

United States

American Association of Suicidology

5221 Wisconsin Avenue NW
Washington, Washington DC 20015
Tel: 202-237-2280; Fax: 202-237-2282
www.suicidology.org
Email: info@suicidology.org

National Mental Health Association

2001 N. Beauregard Street, 12th Floor
Alexandria, VA
22311
Tel: 7.3-684-7722; Fax: 703-684-5968

Safer Child, Inc.

P.O. Box 48151
Spokane, Washington. 99228-1151
Tel: 1-800-784-2433 (Hotline)
www.saferchild.org

Email: lrogers@saferchild.org

Screen for Mental Health Inc.
Washington Street, Suite 304
Wellesley Hills, MA 02481
Tel: 781-239-0071; Fax: 781-431-7447
www.stopasuicide.org
Email: smhinfo@mentalhealthscreening.org

Suicide Prevention Resource Center
Education Development Center
55 Chapel Street
Newton, MA 02458-1060
Fax: 617-969-9186

Washington DC Office
1000 Potomac Street NW, Suite 350
Washington DC, 20007
F: 202-572-3795
www.sprc.org
Email: info@sprc.org

Yellow Ribbon For the Prevention of Teen Suicide
Tel: 303-429-3530
www.yellowribbon.org
Email: ask4help@yellowribbon.org

International

World Health Organization
Regional Office for the Americas
525, 23rd Street, N.W.
Washington, DC. 20037
USA
1-202-974-3000 – telephone
1-202-974-3663 – fax

postmaster@paho.org
Regional Director: Dr. Mirta Roses
www.who.nt/mental_health/prevention/suicide/en

Resources – Websites

Websites

ADDitude Magazine - www.additudemag.com

(The) ADD Warehouse – Books and Resources - www.addwarehouse.com

American Academy of Child & Adolescent Psychiatry - www.aacap.org/publications/factsfam/bipolar

Attention Deficit Disorder Association - www.add.org

Bipolar and Significant Others Foundation – www.bpso.org

(The) Bipolar Child - www.bipolarchild.com

(The) Bipolar Home - www.bipolarhome.org/children

Centre for Suicide Prevention (a program of the Canadian Mental Health Association) – www.suicideinfo.ca

CHADD – Children and Adults with Attention Deficit Disorder - www.chadd.org

Child and Adolescent Bipolar Foundation (CABF) - www.bpkids.org

Childhood Schizophrenia and Bipolar Disorder - www.schizophrenia.com

Depression and Bipolar Support Alliance – www.ndmda.org

Focus Adolescent Services - www.focusas.com/BipolarDisorder

International Association for Suicide Prevention, Suicide Research and Prevention Unit – www.med.uio.no/iasp/index/html

Juvenile Bipolar Research Foundation – www.jbrf.org

National Institute of Mental Health (US) – www.nimh.nih.gov

National Foundation for Depressive Illness – www.depression.org

Not My Kid - www.notmykid.org/parentArticles/DepressionandBipolar

Suicide and Mental Health Association International (SMHAI) – www.suicideandmentalhealthassociationinternational.org

World Health Organization – www.who.nt/mental_health/prevention/suicide/en

www.adhdnews.com

www.addadhdadvances.com

www.BipolarSupporter.com

www.conductdisorders.com

www.medscape.com

www.theinfinitemind.com/mindprogram

www.webmd.com

About The Author

Diane Simon is a journalist and photographer, and has worked on staff and on a freelance basis for many publications. She is also a published poet and has written several non-fictions novels and a series of children's books which are in various stages of publication. Diane currently works as the Promotion and Education Program Coordinator with the Canadian Mental Health Association, Chatham-Kent Branch.

Diane has been married for 24 years to her husband, Brad. They have two sons – Adam, 21, and Cale, who would have celebrated his 20th birthday in November 2006. This book is a testament to Cale's life. Diane began writing this book as therapy – a way of coping with the loss of her son.

Diane is an outspoken advocate for the need for proper, adequate and accessible treatment for persons with mental illness. She is also passionate about the need for public education and awareness concerning mental illness, and the elimination of stigma surrounding mental illness.

Brad and Diane also share their home with a white cat named Stinky, a former barn cat convert, and a beautiful, intelligent and somewhat excitable German Shepherd named Chelsea.

Printed in the United States
54012LVS00001B/7-108